VISIONS OF SUBSTANCE

Visions of Substance

3D Imaging in Mediterranean Archaeology

Edited by
Brandon R. Olson
William R. Caraher

The Digital Press @
The University of North Dakota

Book and Cover Design:
William Caraher

ISBN-13:
978-0692368398 (The Digital Press at The University of North Dakota)

ISBN-10:
0692368396

Acknowledgements

This volume was made possible by the good spirit of the contributors who responded quickly to editorial requests and proof pages. The contributors accepted the premise that their interesting, timely, and, provocative blog posts captured the spirit of informal conversation while, at the same time, could offer substantive scholarly value.

Susan Caraher provided proofreading assistance with this volume. The always flexible staff of The Digital Press at the University of North Dakota ensured that this volume appeared a year after the last blog post. Several papers appeared on the blog and for various reasons do not appear in this volume. They contributed to the arguments and observations in this volme and can be read here: https://mediterraneanworld.wordpress.com/3d-modeling-in-mediterranean-archaeology/

Special thanks go to the College of Arts and Sciences at the University of North Dakota, The Cyprus Research Fund at the University of North Dakota, and the Working Group in Digital and New Media.

CONTENTS

1.
Introduction

Brandon R. Olson

The utilization of 3D tools in archaeology is not a new phenomenon. The use of shading and stippling in artifact illustration, as well as the creation of artifact squeezes and casts, has added a level of three-dimensionality to artifact recording over the last century (Heath 2013; Rick and White 1974). Efforts to update field-recording strategies with 3D solutions date back to the earliest attempts to incorporate terrestrial laser scanners in archaeology (Barceló et al. 2003; Barceló and Vicente 2004; Doneus and Neubauer 2005; Pollefeys et al 2003). Digital reconstruction has been a driving factor for 3D tools within the discipline over the course of the last decade (Sanders 2008, 2011). What is noticeable, however, is a recent proliferation in the adoption of 3D technologies in both the field and lab. The proliferation is evident across the discipline with numerous digital archaeological workshops taking place at institutions such as Brown University, the University of Massachusetts, and Wentworth Institute of Technology among many others. Panels focusing on technology in archaeology draw crowds at the annual meetings of the Archaeological Institute of America, the Society of American Archaeology, and the American Schools of Oriental Research. The development of teleimmersion and cyberarchaeology labs dedicated to specific archaeological sites and landscapes at Duke University and the University of California San Diego demonstrate a significant investment in the development and application of 3D tools.

The trend towards a 3D archaeology is also discernible in print with several peer-review journals dedicating recent issues to digital archaeology (*World Archaeology* (46.1), the *Journal of Eastern Mediterranean Archaeology and Heritage Studies* (2.1 and 2.2), the *Journal of Field Archaeology* (39.2); *Near Eastern Archaeology* (2014), and *Advances in Archaeological Practice* (2014)), while the *Journal of Archaeological Science* has experienced a 300% increase over the last decade in published studies focusing on 3D applications (Olson et al. 2014: 162–163). Despite earlier forays towards the adoption of 3D resources, it is clear that current trends represent a paradigm shift in archaeology (Roosevelt et al. forthcoming). The present collection of essays seeks to provide an accessible primer to both theoretical discussions and practical examples concerning the rapidly-expanding digital archaeological tool kit.

3D Thursday

This conversation originated as a series of guest-authored blog posts on Bill Caraher's *Archaeology of the Mediterranean World* blog (http://mediterraneanworld.wordpress.com). The blog served as a useful vehicle for a conversation about the roles, functions, and value of 3D tools in archaeology because the pace of development in this field is so rapid. The speed with which such a conversation can be disseminated over the Internet and sensitivities that allowed individual contributions to more efficiently toward publication befits the pace of change in some of the technical aspects of our field. New digital 3D resources bring opportunities for new ways to document sites and, of course, opportunities to reflect on the role of technology in archaeology. Over the course of 12 weeks on "3D Thursday," The *Archaeology of the Mediterranean World* (http://mediterraneanworld.wordpress.com/3d-modeling-in-mediterranean-archaeology/) featured a series of contributions from a group of authors describing how a new range of technologies have expanded our ability to produce high-quality 3D images of archaeological sites in Europe and the Mediterranean. The goal was to initiate a conversation among both practitioners of 3D modeling technology and those genuinely interested in these techniques to explore the practical and conceptual limits of these new approaches. After posting a call for papers of sorts, authors were invited to consider four prompts while crafting their contributions:

1. How do we understand the current crop of 3D modeling technologies in the context of the history of archaeological imaging? Are the most optimistic readings of this technology a mere echo of earlier enthusiasm for photography in an archaeological context or is this somehow qualitatively different?

2. Is there an emerging consensus on best practices in 3D imaging of archaeological sites? What are the current limits to this kind of technology and how does this influence the way in which data is collected in the field?

3. How do we understand archival considerations for 3D models and their dependent data? For example, what happens when we begin to prepare

archaeological illustrations from 3D models collected in the field and processed using proprietary software? How do we manage the web of interrelated data so that future archaeologists can understand our decision making?

4. What is the future of 3D modeling in archaeology? At present, the 3D image is useful for illustrating artifacts and – in some cases – presenting archaeological and architectural relationships, but it has yet to prove itself as an essential basis for analysis or as a viable medium for communicating robust archaeological description. Will 3D visualization become more than just another method for providing illustrations for archaeological arguments?

The first three prompts reflect an interest in the way in which the current generation of 3D imaging tools will shape archaeological workflow from the edge of the trowel to final publication. Just as photography promised to revolutionize the field in the late 19th century, efficient and inexpensive 3D modeling tools seemingly offer a simple solution to documenting spatial relationships. The new tools certainly offer remarkable advantages over longstanding techniques for documenting three-dimensional relationships (and displaying them). The process of collecting images from the trench might offer markedly greater efficiently over careful trench-side drawings, but it also eliminates or transforms a process prone to produce important insights from the careful scrutiny of archaeological features in the field. Reproducing the processes responsible for creating 3D images is another issue. Many projects use commercial software that operates with proprietary algorithms and which receive regular updates and improvements. The need to preserve the software, or at least careful technical documentation of the processes used, as well as the raw data processed, is necessary to ensure that the process of documentation is reproducible. Finally, as archives and digital publication opportunities develop there remain serious questions about the durability of these media and the delicate chain that links interpretation to evidence.

The final prompt nudged the contributors to reflect on the future of this kind of technology in archaeological practice. By imagining future directions for this kind of work, we have another avenue to identify present challenges and opportunities. Throughout the 12-week dialogue, the rapidly changing present and approaching future in the world of 3D imaging in archaeology became evident.

Using a blog as the first venue for these contributions was tremendously valuable for a number of reasons. First, as noted above, the rapidity of dissemination was beneficial given the pace of technological change. Second, the established readership base of the *Archaeology of the Mediterranean World* served as a robust pseudo-peer view basis and reader comments often provided feedback for authors as they reworked their contributions for the present volume. Third, scholar, student, and non-academic reader alike had ready access to every contribution, which greatly expanded the audience. Finally, subsequent authors had the added benefit of access to all preceding contributions for use as reference and points of departure. Based on the four prompts outlined above, the articles included here are divided into two sections, theory and practice. The contributions considered theoretically focused consider methodological and analytical issues, as well as the overall impact of 3D tools in archaeology, while the practical works deal primarily with the implementation of specific 3D tools.

Theory

In the first contribution to this section James Newhard, a self-admitted end user of technology in archaeology, examines what type of tool the new breed of digital solutions represent, standard and heavily used tools akin to a common wrench set or overpriced specialty options that will inevitably fall by the wayside. Newhard argues the former and outlines a series of future applications specifically for 3D imagery. Brandon Olson and Ryan Placchetti discuss image based modeling and its 2D byproducts to explore four areas for future development: digital cartography, field recording, object analysis, and digital preservation. Adam Rabinowitz argues that 3D models are more than mere visualizations of an original, rather they are "digital surrogates." Having defined the term as "any digital representation of a work that exists in the physical world," Rabinowitz discusses the relationship between a digital surrogate and the original. He concludes with an outline of four basic principles for publishing and archiving 3D digital surrogates: measurement, raw data, metadata, and process history. In the last contribution to this section, Andrew Reinhard, the director of publications for the American Numismatic Society, provides a unique prospectus for publishing 3D and 4D archaeological data in an attempt to create new and modify preexisting policies to foster the next generation of archaeological publications.

Practice

Using 3D tools to bridge the gap between his work in the field and anyone interested in his efforts, Sebastian Heath discusses his use of 3D modeling on objects from the American Excavations at Kenchreai. The models serve as a viable means to bridge the gap between the producers of 3D models and their consumers by granting greater digital access to the material record. Ethan Gruber uses his recent work at the House of the Faun to demonstrate the analytical value of 3D models and simulations depicting, among other things, sunlight angles and the surrounding environment. The study of such representations altered his (and his collaborator John Dobbins) perception of the ruins, forcing the scholars to develop different interpretations. Rachel Opitz discusses her work at Gabii where 3D tools are harnessed to record and interpret excavation data, craft archaeological arguments, and make these tools part of the publication record. She concludes that a successful adoption of 3D tools requires continued assessment and a willingness to go out on "technical and methodological limbs." Eric Poehler provides an assessment of photomodeling and laser scanning techniques of the Quadriporticus at Pompeii as part of the Pompeii Quadriporticus Project. Guido Nockemann outlines how 3D reconstructions of the Langenbrücker Gate in Lemgo, Germany, as well as archaeological and historical data, can be deployed to present the site to the public in an engaging manner. Finally, in examining an Acheulean handaxe, Brandon Olson, Jody Gordon, Curtis Runnels, and Steve Chomyszak bring 3D imaging full circle when they discuss the scholarly value of 3D printing using three different media: ABS plastic, resin, and powder.

Towards Visions of Substance in Archaeology

While archaeology is entering a new and exciting digital chapter in its history, a consensus has yet to be made on how and what types of digital tools will affect archaeological practices, methods, and interpretations. It bears noting that we do not offer a specific all-encompassing answer here, but with contributions from an eclectic group of digital archaeology practitioners, publishers, numismatists, end users, and graduate students, we hope to add to the nascent dialogue from both theoretical and practical perspectives.

Works Cited

Barceló, J. A., O. De Castro, D. Travet, and O. Vicente. 2003. "A 3D Model of an Archaeological Excavation," in M. Doerr and A. Sarris, eds., *The Digital Heritage of Archaeology: Computer Applications and Quantitative Methods in Archaeology. Proceedings of the 30th Conference, Heraklion, Crete, April 2002.* Crete: Hellenic Ministry of Culture, 85–90.

Barceló, J. A., and O. Vicente. 2004. "Some Problems in Archaeological Excavation 3D Modelling," in K. F. Ausserer, W. Borner, M. Goriany, and L. Karlhuber-Vockl, eds., *Enter the Past: The E-Way into the Four Dimensions of Cultural Heritage. CAA 2003, Computer Applications and Quantitative Methods in Archaeology: Proceedings of the 31st Conference, Vienna, Austria, April 2003.* BAR International Series 1227. Oxford: Archaeopress, 400–404.

Doneus, M., and W. Neubauer. 2005. "3D Laser Scanners on Archaeological Excavations," in S. Dequal, ed., Proceedings of the 20th International Symposium CIPA, Torino 2005. *The International Archives of Photogrammetry, Remote Sensing and Spatial Information Sciences 36.* Turin: Cipa International Symposium, 226–231.

Heath, S. (2013-10-10). "Closing Gaps with Low-Cost 3D," The Archaeology of the Mediterranean World. <http://mediterraneanworld.wordpress.com/2013/10/10/closing-gaps-with-low-cost-3d/>.

Olson, B. R., J. Gordon, C. Runnels, and S. Chomyszak. 2014. "Experimental Three-Dimensional Printing of a Lower Palaeolithic Handaxe: An Assessment of the Technology and Analytical Value," *Lithic Technology* 39: 162–172.

Pollefeys, M., L. Van Gool, M. Vergauwen, K. Cornelis, F. Verbiest, and J. Tops. 2003. "3D Recording for Archaeological Fieldwork," *IEEE Computer Graphics and Applications* 23: 20–27.

7

Rick, J. W. and T. D. White. 1974. "Photography of Obsidian Artifacts: A Useful Alternative," *Newsletter of Lithic Technology* 4: 29.

Roosevelt, C., P. Cobb, E. Moss, B.R. Olson, S. Ünlüsoy. Forthcoming. "Excavation is Destruction Digitization: Advances in Archaeological Practice," *Journal of Field Archaeology.*

Sanders, D. H. 2008. "Why Do Virtual Heritage? Case Studies from the Portfolio of a Long-Time Practitioner," *Archaeology Magazine* (http://www.archaeology.org/online/features/virtualheritage/).

Sanders, D. H. 2011. "Enabling Archaeological Hypothesis Testing in Real Time Using the REVEAL Documentation and Display System," *Virtual Archaeology Review* 2: 89–94.

Theory

2.
3D Imaging in Mediterranean Archaeology:
What are we doing, anyway?

James Newhard

Introduction

I come to the topic of 3D imagery from the perspective largely of the "end user." While I am involved with projects that are capturing and using 3D imagery (such as the Palace of Nestor Linear B project) (Newhard 2013a), my expertise does not lie in this area. As such, my perspective and contributions lie on the level of one who sees 3D imagery largely in the context of its use, and in the broader context of digital applications in archaeology.

To be fair, I have a notorious quirk. I can overlook easily the next great thing (in 1989, I announced to my friends that electronic mail "chatting" was foolish and a waste of time, when a simple telephone bolted onto a wall would do just fine if not better). It usually takes me a period of time between being introduced to a new application, before suddenly—miraculously, even—rediscovering it and seeing not only its utility but near necessity. Similar stories can be told of my first contact with PDAs, multispectral satellite imagery, LiDAR, tablets, smart phones, and GIS.

Some would call this quirk a fault. I would call it a bit of pragmatism. The world is full of toys these days. Innovation is all around us and there is an urge towards the faster, smaller (or bigger), and thinner. Many crave hardware and software that holds more, processes more, and in general finds the answer quicker than ever with more data than ever before considered.

But what is the question? Why do all this? To what end?

Over the past couple of years, there has been an efflorescence of visualization applications. Photogrammetry, 3D imaging, GIS, and other approaches have arrived, to the point that they are beginning to be viewed as a common part of the archaeological toolkit.

I have a couple of questions about these new tools, and will endeavor to supply some answers:

1. In what part of the toolkit do these lie? Are they like my wrench set or more like the $50 thingy I bought for that one project, and will not need again?

2. How are these tools to be used? To collect and present data? To ask questions and evaluate answers? To do a little bit of everything?

3. Do these new tools come with instructions? Are they for everyone to use, or are they specialized tools, best left in the hands of professionals? Who are the professionals, anyway, and how do I either become or obtain one?

To help answer these questions, it is useful to take stock of where we sit in the development of 3D imagery and its applications. I view it as typical of the way technologies have often entered usage; a few brave souls engage in the medium at an early stage, but are rather alone in the world, owing to the steep learning curve of the program and a sense of limited application to questions that are more easily addressed via other means. With time, the software and hardware become more user-friendly and cheaper, allowing more people to experiment and play. Applications of the technology still tend to be "carryovers'" from earlier—in the case of GIS, mylar-layer maps were replaced by digital layers. In the third phase, the software and basic applications have become pervasive enough that people start to become formally trained, and begin to think of the innovation in terms of added value. Again, in the case of GIS—moving from the display of information, to modeling and hypothesis generation, to testing.

In regard to 3D imagery, the Mediterranean world seems to be largely in the second phase of development. Software and imaging capture have become widely accessible, and we have moved beyond the initial "pioneer" phase where a few intrepid scholars spent hours with clunky GUIs to effect rough approximations of reality. The vast majority of applications of 3D imagery still reside in the realm of display and presentation. Incredibly refined and detailed, surely, but largely the digital equivalent of 3D dioramas of bygone ages.

In terms of what kinds of tools we are dealing with, it would appear that the methods are becoming more like a wrench set and less like a specialized, expensive tool rarely used. Increasingly accessible by the rank and file archaeologist, their greater applications beyond basic rendering still remain in the hands of specialists, although forming collaborative teams of people is a time-worn trail of overcoming these hurdles.

Next Steps in 3D

As we gain facility in attaching data to our representations, we should advocate shifting from presentation and display as the end results to one that is involved in dynamic modeling should be engaged. Alternatively, as 3D modeling becomes more commonplace, we should establish systems by which the various parameters that contribute to the model can be formalized and adjustable by the end user. This would resemble the way that current models in GIS can be set up such that an individual need not know the methods to render, yet with a few inputs or choices, be in the role of questioning and discovery. I see several trends in or applications of 3D imagery:

1. Physics/engineering: If we can reconstruct structures in form, we can further use models to explain the relationship between form and function. Using physics, one could use 3D imagery to analyze the strength of structures, thereby shedding light upon a variety of questions—the capabilities of buildings to withstand varying strengths of earthquakes, for example.

2. Metrics: How many pots do we have? The gain from digitizing artifacts in 3D – even the lowly body sherd – is that surface area and thicknesses are readily obtained. For periods where standard sizes of wares are known, one could compute the amount of material recovered of a particular ware type and get a sense of how much is represented. In addition to other information normally collected (number of rims, weights, etc.) this information could be added to provide additional measurables useful for ascribing function to space.

In cases where ware types are ill-defined, such metrics could be useful for retrieving data helpful for classification purposes and addressing issues of specialization and other topics related to the organization of production (Karasik 2012).

3. Viewsheds/cityscapes: With the capacity for building up, we have greater capacity to understand the built landscape. The more that base models mimic actual environmental conditions, the more effective will studies become that draw upon lines of sight and viewsheds.

4. Gaming/engagement/education: The great draw of 3D imagery is in its ability to engage. There is nothing wrong with that—in fact, there is a lot of good. As a form of dissemination that presents in an instant the cumulative knowledge of the research, these applications are powerful. Using 3D as a means to communicate and engage is an important element of the process of dissemination, long overlooked in a discipline that rewards monographs and articles over media that is approachable by the lay person. For both the lay and professional, these products are effective communication devices in their own right.

Overriding all of these applications is the notion of modeling—using the available information to construct a hypothetical that is in some way reflective, iterative, and testable. Ultimately, I view the development of methods in modeling a major goal—the purpose of data collection, after all, is to answer a question and present an interpretation. Modeling provides a means by which data can be structured so as to allow a reflexive approach to hypothesis assessment and re-evaluation. 3D imagery fits within phases of model development, assessment, and eventual dissemination/communication.

Who is going to do this?

We are situated at a time of transformation, when society as a whole is moving from analog to digital, and information has increased in quantity, availability of access, and speed of delivery. For my high school graduation, I received a word processor. I received my first computer as a wedding present immediately after I graduated from college. I made my first website near the end of my graduate studies. Most of my research and organizational skills were "born analog." Not so the next generation of scholars. In the last 20 years, the information age has transformed how we obtain, manipulate, and disseminate our ideas. How has our training of the next generation changed? One would look long and hard for required courses in GIS or database development (although they are encouraged in many places). As I have argued elsewhere (2012, 2013b), we need to think hard about how to bring out formal introduction of the modern tools of our trade into the training of the next generation. Otherwise, we run the risk of having others make the tools for us. Recent comments by Davis and colleagues (2013a, b) have noted that the fields of archaeology and classics are changing in terms of the approaches used, but that our institutional guidelines/curricula are sometimes ill-matched to this new reality. New tools and approaches call for new training, which we have always done. The extent to which we have been beset with innovation, however, calls for serious discussions at the undergraduate and graduate levels in regards to what range of tools the next generation of archaeologist is expected to have and at the professional level in terms of understanding what the outputs of research are and how they are best evaluated.

Archaeology, by its very nature, is a data-laden spatial enterprise. Context is everything, and that context has an x, y, and z coordinate. 3D is inherent to our work of understanding the past. We are drawn to these tools as a way to communicate our interpretations in the most accurate way possible. There are more possibilities beyond description and communication. Just as our earliest work in GIS was to communicate and describe, so too have been our initial forays into the third dimension. The next step, like GIS, is to move in the direction of using these applications to hypothesize, model, test, re-evaluate, and disseminate. Mediterranean archaeology, as both an early and late adopter with its wide array of evidence, stands to contribute greatly to this next phase of discovery. Provided, that is, that we allow ourselves to go there.

Works Cited

Davis, J. L. 2013a. "Barbarians at the Gate," *Archivist's Notebook*. Retrieved from http://nataliavogeikoff.com/2013/09/01/barbarians-at-the-gate/.

Davis, J. L. 2013b. "Barbarians at the Gate: Comments on Comments," *Archivist's Notebook*. Retrieved from: http://nataliavogeikoff.com/2013/09/15/barbarians-at-the-gate-comments-on-comments/.

Karasik, A. 2012. "Computerized Documentation and Analysis of Archaeological Artifacts," paper presented at the Redford Conference in Archaeology. University of Puget Sound, Tacoma, Washington. Oct. 26–27, 2012.

Newhard, J. M. L. 2012. "Convergence," *AIA Geospatial Interest Group.* http://aiageo.wordpress.com.

Newhard, J. M. L. 2013a. "Linear B Archives Project in Full Swing," The *Archaeoinformant.* http://blogs.cofc.edu/thearchaeoinformant/2013/06/21/linear-b-archives-project-in-full-swing/.

Newhard, J. M. L. 2013b. "Archaeology, Humanities, and Data Science," *The Archaeoinformant.* http://blogs.cofc.edu/thearchaeoinformant/2013/08/01/archaeology-humanities-and-data-science/.

3.
A Discussion of the Analytical Benefits of Image Based Modeling in Archaeology

Brandon R. Olson
Ryan A. Placchetti

Introduction

Recent developments in imaged based modeling have ushered in a new era, one in which the primacy of laser scanning as the chief means of three-dimensionally recording archaeologically relevant features and landscapes will be challenged. The release of a handful of image based modeling software platforms, most notably Eos Systems' PhotoModeler Scanner in 2009, Agisoft's PhotoScan in 2010, and Autodesk's 123D Catch in 2012, will transform how Mediterranean archaeologists plan, approach, record, and present their field projects and data for years to come. With the aid of Structure from Motion (SfM) and other comparable photogrammatic algorithms, it is now possible to create accurate and photorealistic 3D models of any target of interest using digital photographs (Figs. 1 and 2). Such a technological breakthrough, however, though capable of transforming archaeological field methods, could, if not utilized correctly, hinder the discipline as well. The purpose of this investigation is to examine the utility and limitations of image based modeling from an archaeological perspective before discussing how 3D recording can become a legitimate analytical tool for the archaeologist, rather than just another means to generate visual aids.

The Utility of Image Based Modeling in Archaeology

A number of recent studies have demonstrated that image based modeling, when the target is prepared and photographed correctly, provides aesthetically pleasing and spatially accurate 3D renderings of archaeological features ranging in size from individual artifacts to entire landscapes (Olson et al. 2013; Remondino 2013; de Reu et al. 2013; Verhoeven 2011). In fact, field tests of PhotoScan Pro revealed that the software can generate models with sub-centimeter spatial accuracy (Forte 2014 and cf. Olson et al. 2013; de Reu et al. 2013). The utility of the technology rests not only with its accurate outputs, but also in its affordability and ease of access. 123D Catch represents an open source option, but even proprietary modeling software packages are cost effective with PhotoScan Pro offering an educational license for $549 USD. Although certain programs are more user-friendly than others, the programs make efforts to present easily navigable user interfaces, especially 123D Catch and PhotoScan Pro. Irrespective of one's technological background, one can achieve a basic level of functional literacy in an afternoon of training with an experienced practitioner. Archaeologists familiar with ESRI's ArcGIS software will appreciate the comparable lack of expertise required to master the full range of functionality offered by 123D Catch and PhotoScan Pro. The aforementioned image based modeling programs offer something that very few archaeologically appropriate technologies do not, they are cheap, easy to use, portable, and yield quality outputs. As such, archaeological projects throughout the eastern Mediterranean such as the Tel Akko Total Archaeology Project (Olson et al. 2013; Killebrew and Olson 2013), the Central Lydia Archaeological Survey, the Athienou Archaeological Project (Toumazou in press), Qazion (Quartermaine et al. 2013), the Jezreel Valley Regional Project, the Pyla-Koutsopetria Archaeological Project, Troy, Çatalhöyük (Forte 2014), Polis-Chrysochous among many others, have implemented the software to address specific needs.

Limitations and Challenges

The current suite of photogrammetric 3D modeling platforms offers an appealing technological addition to any archaeological project. These software packages, however, present a series of specific and broader methodological limitations. The corpus of specific limitations has been discussed elsewhere (Olson et al. 2013; de Reu et al. 2013), but a few select drawbacks bear mentioning. A great deal of the frustration and false starts associated with incorporating image based modeling into an archaeological project can be avoided with a responsible adoption of the technology. First of all, developing a fundamental understanding of how image based modeling approaches reconstruct a spatial environment across a series of photographs, combined with familiarity of proven photographic collection strategies can help to inform the tailoring of a data collection plan for a specific modeling target. Secondly, 3D modeling may not be appropriate to all objects and areas due to technical limitations of the software. Scenes with strings or grass, monochromatic cylindrical objects that lack clearly defined edges when viewed in the round, as well as glass and other transparent surfaces are all problematic features that prevent optimal modeling. Finally, photogrammetric 3D modeling operates best in a controlled environment, but it is perfectly viable in field operations provided that steps have been taken to minimize problematic features and to standardize the scene across the photographic dataset, thus maximizing the computer's efficacy when trying to recreate the spatial environment.

The broader methodological limitations of the software concern its use by archaeologists. Utilization of the technology must be approached with purpose and consideration to ensure that the data are utilized in a way that augments data collection instead of distracting from it. Understanding the investment of effort required to produce and manage a viable 3D dataset requires a basic understanding of how the technology recognizes spatial relationships and the volume and type of data produced at each step of the modeling process. Most importantly, it is necessary to have a clear plan for the role that these models will play within the scheme of a specific archaeological project. In the absence of proper planning, 3D models run the risk of being relegated to curiosity status, functionless byproducts of an overeager adoption of technology or worse, particularly in the context of an ongoing excavation, they might prove to be a waste of valuable time and information if the final product should prove unsuitable for use.

Future Directions: 3D Modeling as an Analytical Tool for Archaeology

As projects continue to adopt this technology, it is important to reflect on how and in what ways image based modeling can become an analytical tool, as opposed to a means of simple archaeological visualization. What is presented below are four avenues that we believe would benefit from quick, accurate, and photorealistic 3D models, and their 2D data derivatives. It is important to note that discussions with a number of colleagues, including Bill Caraher (University of North Dakota), Christopher Roosevelt (Boston University), Jody Gordon (Wentworth Institute of Technology), Ann Killebrew (Pennsylvania State University), and Curtis Runnels (Boston University), helped shape and contextualize what follows.

Digital Cartography
The documentation and dissemination of spatial data is one of the most common concerns of field archaeologists. Traditionally, cartographers seeking to map archaeological features set up a series of datums across an area to be mapped and take a number of measurements in order to produce a hand-drawn map of a feature or site. The process is time intensive and the accuracy of the map is dependent upon the tools used and the skill set of the illustrator. In many cases, upon completion, the map is scanned and opened in a graphics editing program or GIS for digitization. With respect to site and excavation unit level mapping, the benefits of a digital approach are evident, it is faster and more accurate than its manual counterpart. PhotoScan Pro and PhotoModeler Scanner offer a 2D georeferenced orthorectified photograph (henceforth referred to as orthophoto) output where a 3D model is converted into a spatially accurate 2D rendering of the modeled space. The images serve as an ideal basis upon which accurate maps can be digitally drafted.

Field testing has demonstrated that maps of scales ranging from an excavation unit to an entire site created with orthophotos from an image based modeling software are more accurate than maps created with manual drafting methods (Olson et al. 2013; Quartermaine et al. 2014; de Reu et al. 2013). Olson and colleagues (2013) and Quartermaine and colleagues (2014) note that maps of excavation units from Tel Akko were drafted using an orthophoto with sub-millimeter resolution and spatial accuracy averaging 2 cm, while the 3600 sq m site of Qazrin was digitally mapped using an orthophoto with 5 mm resolution and 7 cm accuracy. The two case studies prove that a digital cartographic approach predicated upon the use of orthophotos exported from an image based modeling software provide a time efficient approach to archaeological mapping with unprecedented spatial accuracy.

Field Recording and Volumetrics for Archaeological Excavation
Current documentation strategies of ongoing excavation most often take the form of paper forms, narrative description, and spatial recording in a GIS, which are all 2D based methods that seek to record a 3D space. Attempts to develop a 3D documentation system for excavation have been undertaken with varying degrees of success (Gidding et al. in press; Katsianis et al. 2008; Sanders 2011; Smith and Levy 2012). Despite such at-

tempts, an ideal system, one that is photorealistic and spatially accurate and designed to store excavated data in a 3D environment that enables calculations of volume, an examination of spatial relationships, and is easily updatable, does not exist. It is clear that a digital geographic environment that is spatially controlled and capable of displaying textured 3D data has yet to be developed. ESRI's ArcGIS software and ArcScene do not yet support such an environment. Despite these limitations, the spatial integrity of image based models would serve as an ideal basis for a 3D excavation recording system, given that most of the software packages permit area and volume calculation functions.

Object Analysis

In the past, object analysis has been reliant on either direct physical access to objects or the generally inferior experience of pouring over 2D representations or written descriptions. High-fidelity 3D digital artifacts can help to bridge the gap in quality of data available to researchers by improving the experience of indirect object interaction. Even the physicality of remote object interaction can be partly addressed by incorporating 3D printing technology (Olson et al. this volume, Olson et al. 2014; Forte 2014). The relative immediacy with which digital artifacts can be disseminated across physical boundaries and distances will prove beneficial to scholarly collaboration, while conservation considerations of physical storage space, safe transport, and object deterioration are a non-issue. In a matter of hours, an object discovered in the field can be sent as a 3D model anywhere in the world, expanding the pool of expertise beyond those present at the excavation site to provide a more informed initial analysis.

Digital Preservation

The act of creating a 3D model is a step towards digital preservation. Digital records, provided they are kept up to date with current file format standards, do not deteriorate over time. Rather, they are made resilient by their transferability, duplicability, and finite dimensions. Unlike the locations and objects being recorded, a 3D model is a static representation of its subject at a particular moment in time. Future events that alter the original, whether deleterious or beneficial, make no change in the record. In this sense, the photorealistic 3D model is the documentation tool available to archaeologists that most closely approximates the experience of the original.

While the digital replica is not a truly equal substitute, it can help to mitigate the loss of information and context caused by the forces of nature and destructive human activities such as construction, vandalism, or even further excavation. In extreme cases, where the subject of a model is going to be destroyed and time is limited, as in the case of many rescue archaeology projects, 3D documentation is a fast and reliable way to capture the ephemeral final moments of an archaeological find. In more ideal conditions, the model can also serve as a visual milestone in the life of a subject's archaeological development, providing a record prior to reconstruction or the implementation of protective measures, preserving the find in its most original state and stripped of recent artifice. The opposite also holds true, should the subject of a model fall into disrepair, a 3D record can also provide a basis for restorative work. A 3D model is no replacement for the authentic experience of an original, but it can potentially serve as an enduring record of an artifact, feature, or site in a field burdened, even under the best conditions, by the inevitable degradation of material over time.

Conclusions

As modern archaeologists, we are expected to be thorough and effective custodians of the information with which we have been entrusted. Image based modeling is new, exciting, and scientifically valuable, but should be approached earnestly with clear analytical goals in mind. In terms of realism, 3D models may offer vastly superior visual and spatial representations of objects and areas than traditional 2D methods, but they also represent an analytical resource, provided that diligent consideration of how and why a 3D dataset is created takes place before the first picture is snapped.

The potential to improve mapping methods, spatial recording, object analysis and access, and digital preservation has the potential to transform the discipline. Archaeology is a destructive act because all human works are temporary and attempts to faithfully record and duplicate objects and areas in a digital environment are the closest an archaeologist can come to recreating the moment of discovery. Ready access to 3D modeling provides a reasonably satisfying facsimile of a real world subject when called for, and making permanent what is by definition a temporary state of existence.

The ability to faithfully record, digitally duplicate, and rapidly disseminate photorealistic 3D representations of subjects of archaeological interest is only possible when approached with foresight and only valuable if researchers in the field and in institutions find ways to create effective collaborative spaces. In the absence of collaborative innovation, the archaeological field runs the risk of simply mimicking the results of traditional tools and methods, granted, faster and more accurately, but without realizing the full potential of a digital recording system.

Works Cited

de Reu, J., G. Plets, G. Verhoeven, P. De Smedt, M. Bats, B. Cherretté, W. De Maeyer, J. Deconynck, D. Herremans, P. Laloo, M. Van Meirvenne, and W. De Clercq. 2013. "Towards a Three-Dimensional Cost-Effective Registration of the Archaeological Heritage," *Journal of Archaeological Science* 40: 1108–1121.

Forte, M. 2014. "3D Archaeology: New Perspectives and Challenges—The Example of Çatalhöyük," *Journal of Eastern Mediterranean Archaeology and Heritage Studies* 2: 1–29.

Gidding, A., Y. Matsui, T. E. Levy, T. DeFanti, and F. Kuester. In press. "ArchaeoSTOR: A Data Curation System for Research on the Archaeological Frontier," *Future Generation Computer Systems*.

Katsianis, M., S. Tsipidis, K. Kotsakis, and A. Kousoulakou. 2008. "A 3D Digital Workflow for Archaeological Intra-Site Research Using GIS," *Journal of Archaeological Science* 35: 655–667.

Killebrew, A. E., and B. R. Olson. 2014. "The Tel Akko Total Archaeology Project: New Frontiers in the Excavation and 3D Documentation of the Past," in P. Bielinski, M. Gawlikowski, R. Kolinski, D. Lawecka, A. Soltysiak, and Z. Wygnanska, eds., *Proceedings of the 8th International Congress on the Archaeology of the Ancient Near East*. Wiesbaden: Harrassowitz, 559–574.

Olson, B. R., R. A. Placchetti, J. Quartermaine, and A. E. Killebrew. 2013. "The Tel Akko Total Archaeology Project (Akko, Israel): Assessing the Suitability of Multi-Scale 3D Field Recording in Archaeology," *Journal of Field Archaeology* 38: 244–262.

Olson, B. R., J. M. Gordon, C. Runnels, S. Chomyszak. 2014. "Experimental Three-Dimensional Printing of a Lower Palaeolithic Handaxe: An Assessment of the Technology and Analytical Value," *Lithic Technology* 39: 162-172.

Quartermaine, J., B. R. Olson, and A. E. Killebrew. 2014. "Image-Based Modeling Approaches to 2D and 3D Digital Drafting in Archaeology at Qazrin and Tel Akko: Two Case Studies," *Journal of Eastern Mediterranean Archaeology and Heritage Studies* 2: 110-127.

Quartermaine, J, B. R. Olson, and M. Howland. 2013. "Using Photogrammetry and Geographic Information Systems (GIS) to Draft Accurate Plans of Qazion," *Journal of Eastern Mediterranean Archaeology and Heritage Studies* 1: 169–174.

Remondino, F. 2013. "Worth a Thousand Words- Photogrammetry for Archaeological 3D Surveying," in R. S. Opitz and D. C. Cowley, *Interpreting Archaeological Topography: 3D Data, Visualisation, and Observation. Occasional Publications of the Aerial Archaeology Research Group* 5. Oxford: Oxbow, 115–122.

Sanders, D. H. 2011. "Enabling Archaeological Hypothesis Testing in Real Time Using the REVEAL Documentation and Display System," *Virtual Archaeology Review* 2: 89–94

Smith, N. G., and T. E. Levy. 2012. "Real-time 3D Archaeological Field Recording: ArchField, an Open-Source GIS System Pioneered in Southern Jordan," *Antiquity* 86: http://antiquity.ac.uk/projgall/smith331

Toumazou, M. K., D. B. Counts, E. W. Averett, J. M. Gordon, and P. N. Kardulias. In press. "Shedding Light on the Cypriot Rural Landscape: Investigations of the Athienou Archaeological Project in the Malloura Valley, Cyprus, 2011–2013," *Journal of Field Archaeology.*

Verhoeven, G. J. J. 2011. "Taking Computer Vision Aloft—Archaeological Three-Dimensional Reconstructions from Aerial Photographs with PhotoScan," *Archaeological Prospection* 18: 67–73.

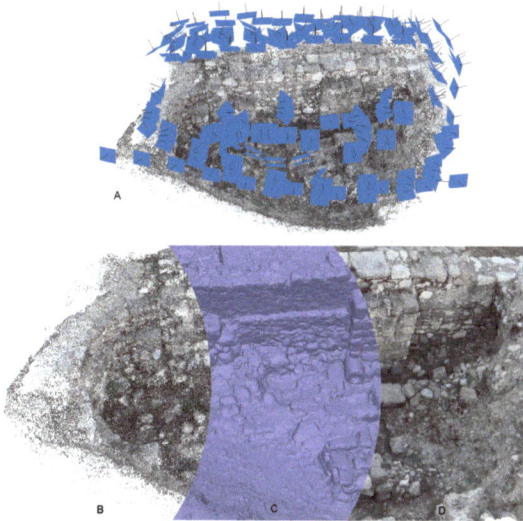

Figure 1: Image of a secondary apse from a Late Roman basilica at Polis-Chrysochous, Cyprus depicting the three stages of creating a 3D model using an image based modeling technique: A) The automatic alignment of photographs; B) A 3D point cloud; C) The untextured 3D model; D) The final textured model. Thanks to Bill Caraher for permission to design and present this image.

Figure 2: Cutaway showing the point cloud, untextured model, and textured model of an Acheulean handaxe. Thanks to Curtis Runnels for granting access to this artifact.

4.

The Work of Archaeology in the Age of Digital Surrogacy

Adam Rabinowitz

Introduction

I am very glad to have the opportunity to contribute to this volume because its contents, taken as a whole, demonstrate with particular clarity that field archaeology is at a turning-point in its engagement with 3D visualization. A decade ago, a collection of discussions of 3D technologies in archaeology would have been concerned mainly with computer-aided virtual reconstructions and immersive environments or with the use of laser scanners. This series, however, has highlighted an emerging common interest in the use of computational photography to create photorealistic 3D representations of archaeological material.

Certain contributions to this volume emphasize the way new software and methods have lowered the bar for the creation of high-quality 3D or 2.5D models of physical objects. James Newhard suggests that these tools are becoming wrenches in the standard archaeologist's toolkit, and I think this trend is likely to intensify over the next decade, especially as drone-based photography becomes a matter of course. Such tools offer two enormous advantages: the enrichment of data collection in the field, which in turn enhances the archaeologist's interpretive process (a point made by Brandon Olson and Ryan Placchetti, Rachel Opitz, and Eric Poehler); and the ability to make distant objects available for scholarly autopsy, as Dimitri Nakassis argues in his post on Reflectance Transformation Imaging. As an added benefit, quick, cheap 3D representations created through computational photography provide a new way for mass audiences to engage with the physicality and materiality of objects, both in an academic publishing environment, as Andrew Reinhard enthusiastically affirms, and, as Sebastian Heath demonstrates, in connection with active excavations and museum collections as well. That last point was recently driven home by the public launch of the Smithsonian X 3D project (3d.si.edu), which presents models of objects in the institute's collections, complete with downloads suitable for 3D printing (though it must be noted that most of this data was captured by more traditional laser scanning).

These contributions also highlight the extraordinary extent to which this shift has been driven by just two recent developments: the popularization of the Polynomial Texture Mapping algorithm developed by Tom Malzbender (Malzbender et al. 2001) (http://www.hpl.hp.com/research/ptm/), in large part through the efforts of Cultural Heritage Imaging (http://culturalheritageimaging.org/); and the rapid improvement of the algorithms that produce 3D models using structure-from-motion (sometimes casually referred to as "photogrammetry"), represented particularly by Agisoft's Photoscan software (http://www.agisoft.ru/products/photoscan) and Autodesk's 123DCatch app (http://www.123dapp.com/catch). Many of us had carried out experiments with computational photography and structure-from-motion in the early 2000s (Fig. 1) (see also Tschauner and Siveroni Salinas 2007; Rabinowitz et al. 2007), but the new tools have transformed a laborious manual process involving a certain amount of technical expertise in both image capture and transformation into a fully automated workflow that even corrects for the defects of the photographer (see now De Reu et al. 2013 and Olson et al. 2013).

The attraction is powerful: unlike conjectural 3D reconstructions or the pure geometry offered by laser-scan point clouds, computational photography seems to promise unmediated access to the physical reality of existing material remains. As Heath points out (this volume), and as can be seen even more dramatically in the recent use of Google Glass to capture a 3D digital model of a head of Marcus Aurelius in the Walters Art Gallery (http://toddblatt.blogspot.com/2013/06/3d-scanning-through-glass.html), the technology also offers significant possibilities for open access and democratization. Anyone with a smartphone with a camera and a few minutes can create a passable 3D model of an archaeological object or work of art and post it online. The examples below give a sense of the variability in the effort required and the quality of the results. Figure 2 is a model of a cast of the Belvedere Torso in the Blanton Museum of Art, created in the space of about five minutes with 16 hasty photographs taken with an iPhone and processed with AutoDesk's 123D Catch app. Figure 3 is a model of an inscription found at Troy and now held by the UT Department of Classics—this more careful representation involved 37 photographs and a light source, and took about 20 minutes to create, again with 123DCatch.

Digital Surrogates

I have called these 3D digital objects "models" and "representations," but they are perhaps more accurately described as "digital surrogates." "Digital surrogate" is a term of art used in the libraries and archives to refer to any digital representation of a work that exists in the physical world (a thumbnail, a metadata record, a digital image). More commonly, however, the term indicates a faithful digital copy that seeks to represent an analogue original as accurately and in as much detail as possible: "By definition, a surrogate can be used in place of the original. If a surrogate is electronic, the same files can be used both internally (to protect the original when the surrogate is of sufficient quality and accuracy to stand in place of the original), and externally (to provide wider access for those who might otherwise be unable to view or study an original)" (Grycz 2006: 34).

Not all surrogates are "of sufficient quality" to serve as substitutes for originals, of course, and there is still a lot of discussion about the extent to which even the highest-resolution scan can replace contact with an original document (the term is almost always used to talk about two-dimensional objects like manuscripts or photographs). Nevertheless, the notion of the digital surrogate reflects an underlying assumption that a digital reproduction ought to be able to stand in for the real thing—and therefore it is particularly appropriate for 3D digital objects that seek to reproduce the visual and spatial characteristics of objects in the real world. A good surrogate is not merely a copy: it is supposed to provide, in some sense, access to the original, now made ubiquitous and opened for inspection on a level of detail that the original itself might not allow. Olson and Placchetti (this volume) make just such a point in their reflections on the use of 3D models elsewhere in this volume.

Popular accounts of the rise of computational photography already treat the surrogate as if it provided access to the reality of the physical original. In the November/December 2013 issue of *Archaeology*, for example, a brief article on the use of drone photography in Peru concludes with the excavator's somewhat breathless claim that "[y]ou can model every single stone" of a site (Swaminathan 2013). And even sober NPR correspondent Robert Siegel, covering the Smithsonian 3D project, was compelled to ask whether digital reproduction techniques will become so good that they will allow the creation of perfect "forgeries" that are indistinguishable from the originals (http://www.npr.org/blogs/alltechconsidered/2013/11/13/245053489/print-your-own-revolutionary-war-boat-in-3-d). But when we look at these surrogates, are we really being afforded closer contact with reality? Or do these exciting, rapid, "disruptive" (to use a word very much of the moment) changes mask some underlying epistemological and methodological problems? I think it is worth attempting to establish a theoretical framework to help us understand not only the benefits conferred by these technological advances, but also what is really happening as we leap from original to digital surrogate.

From Original to Digital Surrogate: A Theoretical Framework

A starting point for this discussion is offered by Walter Benjamin's oft-cited essay "The Work of Art in the Age of Mechanical Reproduction," in which the cultural critic reacts to the impact of new technologies on the social role of Art (with a capital "A"). These new technologies made possible the large-scale dissemination of faithful representations of unique artworks and the exploration of visual phenomena that could not be captured through ordinary perception. Benjamin was concerned that such reproductions would destroy what he called the "aura" of original, "authentic" works of art: that is, the artwork's "presence in time and space, its unique existence at the place where it happens to be" (Benjamin 1968: 220). The availability of copies, mass-produced for mass consumption, led to "the desire of contemporary masses to bring things 'closer' spatially and humanly, which is just as ardent as their bent toward overcoming the uniqueness of every reality by accepting its reproduction." "Every day," he continues, "the urge grows stronger to get hold of an object at very close range by way of its likeness, its reproduction" (223).

The essay was published in 1936, and the new technologies that inspired Benjamin's concerns were photography and its offshoot, cinema. But he might as well be speaking of the 3D representations of ancient "originals" that many of the contributions to this volume focus on. The mechanical reproduction has given way to the digital surrogate—a representation of an analog original in the form of the ones and zeroes of binary code—but less has changed in the last 80 years than one might expect, especially since these digital surrogates continue to be generated with the same old new technology of photography.

The effects of digital surrogates mirror those Benjamin ascribes to photography and film: they distance us from the unique physical thing-ness of that which they represent while allowing us to manipulate reality in ways that the original would not permit. Compare, for example, his claim that the "enlargement of a snapshot does not simply render more precise what in any case was visible, though unclear: it reveals entirely new structural formations of the subject" (236) with Eric Poehler's statement (this volume) that 3D surrogates of Pompeian architecture allow views that would not be physically possible for an observer present in person. Or compare the 3D isolation of stratigraphic sequences that Opitz (this volume) describes, free from extraneous layers, excavators, plants, tools, etc., with Benjamin's comment on the invisibility in movies of the cameras, lights, and personnel needed to make them: "[t]he equipment-free aspect of reality here has become the height of artifice" (233).

Two fundamental points emerge from Benjamin's critique. One is that a surrogate is not the original, nor does it represent reality: it is the product of "artifice," of techniques and processes that are themselves not visible in the end product. The other is that photography is fundamentally different from earlier two-dimensional copying techniques: "for the first time in the process of pictorial reproduction, photography freed the hand of the most important artistic functions which henceforth devolved only upon the eye looking into a lens" (219). He has in mind techniques like woodcuts and engravings, which produced multiple copies of a single original. The engraved original itself might be a reproduction of an existing work of art—but in that case, too, the engraving was also an artistic interpretation (Fig. 4), not a straightforward reproduction, and the product of the creativity and skill of the engraver (Fyfe 2004).

The tension between original and reproduction, art and artifice, access and authenticity, is not a new one in Mediterranean archaeology. In fact, long before the discovery of photography, the birth of ancient art history was entwined with the creation of 3D surrogates through increasingly mechanical means. In the Renaissance and the early Baroque period, sculptors like Bernini prided themselves on their ability to imitate or add to ancient sculptures, and gem-cutters produced new intaglio gemstones based on Greek and Roman originals. By the 17th century, however, broader interest in Classical Antiquity and its iconography led to a market for casts of impressions from the ancient gems themselves. These casts were collected in dactyliothecae that served as iconographic encyclopedias (Knüppel 2009) (http://www.daktyliothek.de/). Dactyliothecae functioned in the same way as the digital 3D surrogates we have been discussing: they allowed the close study of 1:1 representations of absent objects to extract "authentic" visual information, and they offered mass access to originals that were scattered among different collections across Europe. At the same time, large-scale ancient sculpture was also being cast in plaster, again to allow the experience of the "real" (or hyper-real!) form and volume of absent originals and to permit the centralized collection of works otherwise dispersed in geographic space (Borbein 2000) (http://www.digitalsculpture.org/casts/borbein/).

The mechanical reproduction processes involved meant that casts of gem impressions and sculptures were usually at a scale of more or less 1:1, which added to the sense of access to an original. That impression was reinforced by artifice as well: casts of sculpture could be acquired with various finishes meant to evoke marble patinas, different stones, even metals. Here, however, we move from authenticity to verisimilitude—that is, the finishes did not necessarily reproduce the appearance of the original, but evoked the way an object like this was supposed to look. The distinction between truth and truthiness extended to the form of sculptural casts as well. Because so many of the sculptures reproduced were already Roman "reproductions" of Greek statues, they existed in multiple exemplars, each of which might have better preserved components (one might have a head but no arms, another arms but no head, etc.). Some casts were thus actually amalgams of the best-preserved parts of different originals. In other cases, minor additions or changes were made to better suit the appearance of the reproduction to the tastes or expectations of the consumer. The introduction of these modifications during the technical process that created the cast is invisible to the viewer. Instead, changes made to make a cast look more "Classical" shape in turn our notion of what the "Classical" is supposed to look like. For all the use of mechanical reproduction, then, these apparently straightforward surrogates have a problematic relationship with their originals.

If casts offer a Victorian analogy for the 3D digital surrogates created with structure-from-motion algorithms, the venerable paper-pulp epigraphic squeeze is the analog ancestor of the reflectance transformation image.

Again, the crucial quality of the squeeze is its mechanical reproduction, at a 1:1 scale, of the physical surface features of the original, without the interpretive intervention involved in the publication of measurements and transcriptions. Squeezes were generally produced by and for scholars, and were not subject to the sorts of interventions that casts are. On the other hand, the quality of a given squeeze depends on the technical abilities and equipment of the squeeze-maker. Like casts, then, squeezes are not simply "physical surrogates" for originals, but objects of artifice derived from originals through specific processes mediated by their creators and often conditioned by preconceived ideas about how the final product should look.

I have spent this time on physical 3D surrogates for two reasons. First, they highlight the importance of scale and measurement for the usefulness of a surrogate. Squeezes and casts are valuable precisely because they are 1:1 in scale, and can thus allow measurement of the original by proxy. Second, as Benjamin argues for mechanical reproductions in general, they have a problematic relationship with their originals. On one hand, some surrogates have preserved information about originals that are now lost or damaged—early examples of the LOCKSS (Lots of Copies Keeps Stuff Safe) principle. And squeezes continue to be used by epigraphers for off-site study of inscriptions, even when the original still exists. On the other hand, plaster casts have had a generally unsuccessful run. After being introduced as better representations of the reality of the originals than the originals themselves in the 18th century, they had fallen out of favor by the middle of the 20th, perhaps in part as a result of the concern of critics like Benjamin with authenticity and "aura." Many collections were destroyed; others persisted in a sort of half-life as curiosities, but not as resources for scholarly inquiry.

Fundamentally, casts have not been able to maintain their initial value as "cultural capital," in sociologist Pierre Bourdieu's sense. This is in part due to their diffusion, which makes it difficult to control their use as symbols of distinction: the cultural capital provided by a full-scale cast of the Farnese Hercules is somewhat diminished by the existence of the SkyMall version (http://www.skymall.com/the-farnese-hercules-statue/NG-32438.html). But it is also due to the opacity of the process by which they were created and the lack of information about the context of that creation. This is true of all varieties of physical 3D surrogates. A cast made for the tastes of the commercial market may not be trustworthy for academic research, and a squeeze made by an untrained beginner may be a poor representation of the original.

Conclusions and Future Directions

The history of these physical surrogates and Benjamin's critique of mechanical reproduction offer us a foundation for a more considered approach to digital 3D surrogates. I would like to conclude with two starting points for further theorization and discussion.

First, I think it will be of fundamental importance to remember that the digital 3D model is not a true surrogate for the original, even when derived from photographs. This is particularly true for models of archaeological remains in the process of excavation, which will never again be available for first-hand autopsy. I would argue, therefore, that it will be critical not to throw out the handicraft in archaeological documentation—the measured hand-drawn plans and interpretive sketches that, like engravings of artworks, admit that they are representations that seek to highlight the choices and ideas of the creator, and do not claim to be mechanical reproductions of objective reality. Optiz (in this volume) makes the same observation in her post, and I think it is supported by a growing body of research on the special ways in which our brains interact with drawing surfaces and writing instruments (we need more studies on haptics and embodied cognition in archaeology: http://www.intechopen.com/books/advances-in-haptics/digitizing-literacy-reflections-on-the-haptics-of-writing). It would be a grave mistake to lose the skills necessary to create interpretive drawings in our rush to adopt quick, easy, and powerful computational-photographic methods.

Second, I would like to propose a set of four basic principles for publication and archiving to ensure the future scholarly usefulness of the 3D digital surrogates derived from computational photography. Some of these are already in place, at least in some forward-looking projects; others will require the development of new tools. All of them, I think, will be extremely important as computational-photographic methods become more powerful, more democratic, and more black-boxy for most users.

1) Measurement. To ensure that scholars can reuse the 3D data you are

generating, the models have to include some user-accessible information about scale and units, ideally in the form of both in-interface measurement tools and a platform-independent marker (like a clearly-marked meter stick included in the image). This seems like an easy one, but it is trickier than it looks. Andrew Reinhard (in this volume) noted that keeping scale constant would be hard across different publication formats, and the models of the portico and the marble feet in Heath's contribution highlight the effects of lack of scale. When we consult 2D documentation, we frequently make our own measurements using either the scale statements or the scale bars provided in the illustration. In order to be truly useful, 3D model-delivery platforms must offer the same opportunities (Adobe's 3D PDFs include a measurement tool, but the basic Unity interface and p3d.in do not).

2) Raw data. I feel that we are ethically bound to provide not only models, but our original raw data for reuse wherever possible. The importance of this—and the problems with access that turns out to be open in name only—has been reinforced by a recent case involving CyArk and proprietary control of laser-scanning data (for details, see the original post: http://rapidlasso.com/2013/04/14/can-you-copyright-lidar/, with additional discussion: http://lists.okfn.org/pipermail/open-archaeology/2013-October/thread.html). These digital objects are at least one step closer to the reality of the original, and they also make it possible to reprocess the data as more powerful tools and algorithms come online.

3) Metadata. The raw data, of course, are of little use without comprehensive metadata that not only describe file formats, creation dates, etc., but also indicate what those raw data represent. This is going to be especially important for the enormous batches of photographs generated for the purposes of computational photography. It is great if the final model has metadata that tell us it is a Pompeiian building—but I would argue that we need to ensure that every photograph in the sequence has metadata that describes at least the technical details of the photographic file AND the basic identifying information for the object or monument it represents AND the context of its creation, including date, actors, project, etc.

4) Process history. A 3D digital surrogate is not the same as the physical original not just because of its format, but because it is the product of the computational manipulation of a series of intervening digital surrogates, whether photographs or laser scans. Our ability to trust and use the model

depends on our ability to trace—and ideally to walk back—the processes by which it was generated, including parameters, assumptions, and fudges. Systems must be in place to capture and store this information so that users in the future will understand how a model was produced and therefore how it can or cannot be used. Cultural Heritage Imaging has made a lot of progress toward this goal with their work on empirical provenience and the "digital lab notebook," (http://culturalheritageimaging.org/Technologies/Digital_Lab_Notebook/) and I would like to see similar practices adopted by all archaeological and heritage projects that use computational photography.

These principles come with a handy acronym: MRMPH, recognizable as the noise you make when you are asked a question while taking a really large bite of something or while just waking up (I have never been good at generating slick acronyms). In all seriousness, though, the application of these principles to the publication and archiving of 3D digital surrogates will mark a watershed in archaeology: it will be the first time since the birth of our discipline that the archaeological record will grow richer, rather than poorer, with age, since new algorithms and software will permit the ever-more precise and accurate reprocessing of digital photographs for the extraction of 3D information. As 3D printing takes off, we will also have a new opportunity to recreate the archaeological record through widely available physical surrogates, which offer their own advantages for accessibility and interpretation. All this will be possible, however, only if we recognize with Benjamin that reproductions cannot be stand-ins for originals, and acknowledge that digital surrogates in particular have their own independent reality as objects or works requiring their own documentation and explanation (Manovich 2001; Cameron 2007).

Works Cited

Benjamin, W. 1968 [1936]. "The Work of Art in the Age of Mechanical Reproduction," Reprinted in H. Arendt, ed., *Illuminations. Essays and Reflections*, translated by H. Zohn. New York: Schocken Books, 217–251.

Borbein, A. 2000. "Zur Geschichte der Wertschätzung und Verwendung von Gipsabgüssen antiker Skulpturen (insbesondere in Deutschland und in Berlin)," in H. Lavagne and F. Queyrel, eds., *Les moulages de sculptures antiques et l'histoire de l'archéologie. Actes du colloque international Paris, 24 octobre 1997.* Geneva, 29–43. Text translated by B. Frischer. Available at: http://www.digitalsculpture.org/casts/borbein/.

Cameron, F. 2007. "Beyond the Cult of the Replicant - Museums and Historical Digital Objects: Traditional Concerns, New Discourses," in F. Cameron and S. Kenderdine, eds., *Theorizing Digital Cultural Heritage. A Critical Discourse.* Cambridge: The MIT Press, 49–76.

de Reu, J., G. Plets, G. Verhoeven, P. De Smedt, M. Bats, B. Cherrett, W. De Maeyer, J. Deconynck, D. Herremans, P. Laloo, M. Van Meirvenne, and W. De Clercq. 2013. "Towards a Three-Dimensional Cost-Effective Registration of the Archaeological Heritage," *Journal of Archaeological Science* 40: 1108–1121.

Fyfe, G. 2004. "Reproductions, Cultural Capital, and Museums: Aspects of the Culture of Copies," *Museum and Society* 2, 1: 47–67.

Grycz, C. J. 2006. "Digitising Rare Books and Manuscripts," in L. W. MacDonald, ed., *Digital Heritage.* London: Elsevier, 33–68.

Knüppel, H. C. 2009. *Daktyliotheken: Konzepte einer historischen Publikationsform.* Ruhpolding: Rutzen.

Malzbender, T., D. Gelb, and H. Wolters. 2001. "Polynomial Texture Maps," in L. Pocock, ed., *Proceedings of the 28th Annual Conference on Computer Graphics and Interactive Techniques.* New York: ACM Press, 519–528. Available at http://www.hpl.hp.com/research/ptm/papers/ptm.pdf.

Manovich, L. 2001. *The Language of New Media.* Cambridge: The MIT Press.

Olson, B. R., R. A. Placchetti, J. Quartermaine, and A. E. Killebrew. 2013. "The Tel Akko Total Archaeology Project (Akko, Israel): Assessing the Suitability of Multi-Scale 3D Field Recording in Archaeology," *Journal of Field Archaeology* 38: 244–262.

Rabinowitz, A., S. Eve, and J. Trelogan. 2007. "Precision, Accuracy, and the Fate of the Data: Experiments in Site Recording at Chersonesos, Ukraine," in J. Clark and E. Hagemeister, eds., *Digital Discovery: Exploring New Frontiers in Human Heritage, CAA 2006*. Budapest: Archeolingua, 243–256.

Swaminathan, N. 2013. "Drones Enter the Archaeologist's Toolkit," *Archaeology* 66, 6: 22.

Tschauner, H., and S. Siveroni Salinas. 2007. "Stratigraphic Modeling and 3D Spatial Analysis Using Photogrammetry and Octree Spatial Decomposition," in J. Clark and E. Hagemeister, eds., *Digital Discovery: Exploring New Frontiers in Human Heritage, CAA 2006*. Budapest: Archeolingua, 256–270.

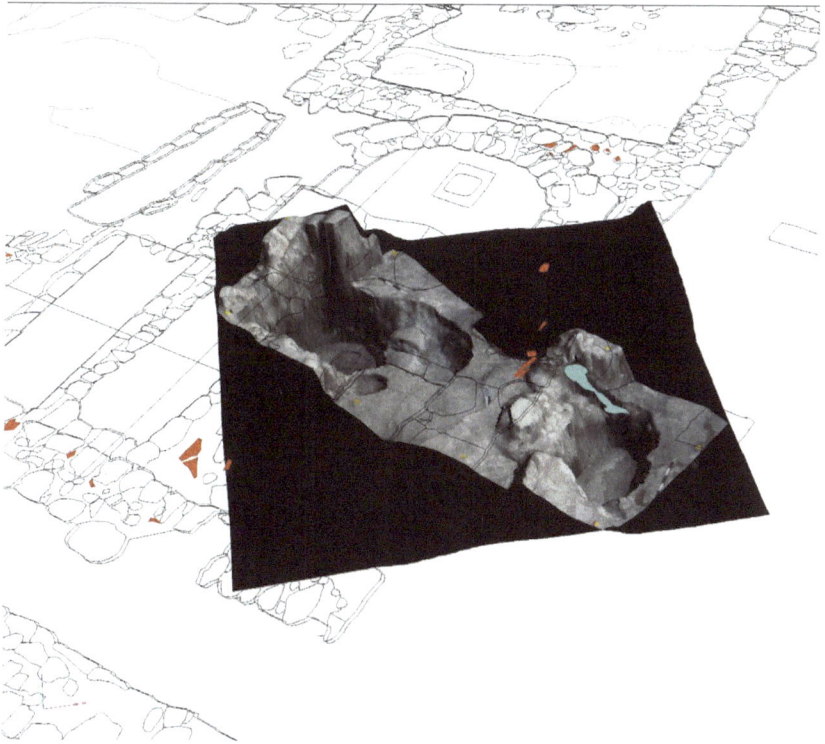

Figure 1: 3D model of bedrock features uncovered at Chersone-sos in the 2006 field season, created from photos with Photo-Modeler Pro. The model was georeferenced in ESRI's ArcScene, and then exported to a 3D PDF using Adobe Acrobat 9 Professional Extended (sadly no longer available).

Figure 2: Belvedere Torso

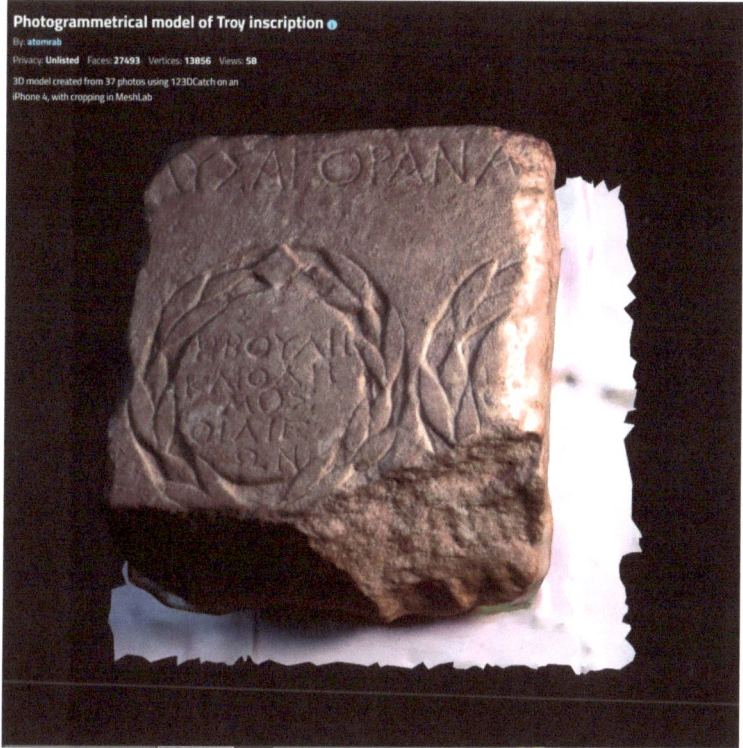

Figure 3: Photogrammetrical model of Troy inscription

Figure 4: Engraving depicting an intaglio gem from von Stosch's collection, from Winckelmann's 1760 publication. This "digital surrogate" of the printed illustration is housed in the Arachne database of the German Archaeological Institute, where it is also linked to records associated with the publication, the original gem, and casts of gem impressions: http://arachne.uni-koeln.de/item/objekt/207726

5.
Three- and Four-Dimensional Archaeological Publication

Andrew Reinhard

Introduction

I have been the Director of Publications for the American School of Classical Studies at Athens (ASCSA) for just over three years, and am responsible for publishing our quarterly journal, *Hesperia*, as well as excavation monographs for Ancient Corinth, the Athenian Agora, and affiliated sites, plus *Hesperia Supplements* on special archaeological topics, as well as guidebooks and limited series. The views that I express in this contribution are my own, but it is my hope that various official ASCSA boards and committees will agree with me on at least some of these points, creating new policy and modifying the old, as the press works with archaeologists to create the next generation of archaeological publications.

Historically archaeology has been limited (and some could argue continues to be limited) to two-dimensional publication in print. Journals and monographs are traditionally printed and include commentary, catalogue, concordances, various front and back matter, tables, photographs of objects and of sites (mostly black-and-white, but occasionally color), drawings (plans, sections, profiles, etc.), and maps. In recent years, some journals and books have been released as "digital editions" onto platforms such as JSTOR, Cambridge Journals Online, and through various publisher websites. By and large, these digital editions do not take advantage of any of the possibilities afforded by appearing on the Internet, being merely one-to-one digital reproductions of their original print counterparts. Readers can choose to read articles in print or on-screen. Those readers who opt to read on-screen do so either because they are traveling (or are away from their offices/libraries), or because their libraries only have digital versions of publications. These digital publications are either served online in an HTML page-view or as PDFs, occasionally in other formats, rarely sharable or even printable because of outdated digital rights management (DRM) and copy protection "safeguards." In the case of PDFs (and devices and apps used to read them), readers are generally unaware of added functionality offered to these "flat" publications: document-searching, bookmarking, note-taking, emailing, etc. I argue that for the average reader of archaeological scholarship, they are, and will remain oblivious, stuck in Flatland, unable to comprehend all the practicality that extra-dimensional publication can offer (and is already beginning to offer).

Taking the aforementioned elements of print publication of archaeological material, let us first apply a 3D filter, followed by a fourth-dimensional one:

Text

It would seem obvious that text is text and that it is by its very nature two-dimensional. The writer writes what the reader reads. Writing an article or a monograph is a one-way form of communication. However, if one extracts this text from its two-dimensional setting and places it online, that text has the native ability to become something more. The content gains context. One can embed links reaching out to Open Access data repositories for people- and place-data. Making this publication available online also facilitates linking in the opposite direction, making the author's content discoverable by anyone in the world, provided the text is given a stable URI (Uniform Resource Identifier). Widgets are now available that enable readers to roll over a placename and retrieve a pop-up window with a map and data along with a clickable link. In time, I hope to see a similar widget crawl through bibliographies and citations in notes, allowing readers to reference cited material as they proceed through the book or article. How often have you, as a reader, wished to check a reference or look up a place, but have instead put it off, not wanting to trek to the library or even run a Google search? Embedding these links and reading tools are a service to readers and are becoming increasingly easy to implement from an author's/publisher's perspective.

This "multi-dimensional" text takes what is good about the printed word, and adds practical improvements that help deliver more robust content more quickly to the reader: Note-taking on the printed page is limited to the space in the margins or between the lines. Note-taking on a digital document allows for notes of massive length that can then be emailed/shared outside of that document. If you lose your book, you lose your notes. Digital editions allow you to save a "clean" copy as well as an annotated copy, and if you email/share your comments, losing your annotated copy is only an inconvenience, not a disaster.

What if we could go one step further, making the author's primary text "four dimensional?" In physics, three dimensions incorporate length, width, and depth. Add time to a 3D thing, and it now has a fourth dimension. All objects exist in space-time, and as the arrow of time moves us forward year by year, those 3D objects change. While this observation will be more readily applied to imaging artifacts, we can apply the four-dimensional concept to an author's text.

A published monograph is like a finished temple. It is as good as the makers can produce at the time. As time moves along, things happen to the building. It can receive additions. It can be shored up. It might be demolished, lending its parts as spolia to other structures in future times. As archaeologists, we can also reduce the structure to its individual parts, seeing how the whole was completed, and also understanding how that building changed over time, from realized vision to revered monument, or derelict footprint. It is a misconception that a published monograph or article is the "final publication" of archaeological material. Upon publication, that text (and its related content of photos, maps, tables, etc.) becomes the starting point for rigorous discussion and dialogue. In the past, some journals have published rebuttals to earlier articles in later issues, a kind of time-delayed chess match. By integrating online publication with mature social networking/commentary technology, those discussions can be opened to a global audience. Should a counter-argument be made successfully, it is also possible for the author to make a change to the main text, or to add new bibliography, and to update notes over time, keeping current with future scholarship. The content of the published piece must change over time, and opening that content up to scrutiny can help to preserve and promote excellent scholarship or to mend, repair, or demolish research.

Seeing text as four dimensional also allows the readers to uncover the foundations of an archaeological publication. In the instances of preliminary excavation reports or "final" reports of a class of objects from a site, I would strongly urge authors to provide their readers with complete data sets. This data can be checked, and can be used as a reference by readers. Should errors be discovered in the math and logic of tables, these can be corrected right away. And should there be a difference of opinion between author and reader, the data can be consulted, and a dialogue started. With traditional publication, the reader is presented with the author's interpretation of the data, and that interpretation might or might not be reliable and might include biases, either conscious or unconscious. Opening up the data, and opening up the dialogue can help an author's argument become more objective.

Tables

A mixture of text and graphical elements (i.e., lines, shading, etc.), tables convey quantifiable data to support the author's arguments, and to also relay in a readable form what was found over the course of a season, or of a decades-long excavation. In two-dimensional publishing, the table is printed on the page, or over one or several spreads, with a caption, headings, and notes. In 3D online publishing, that table becomes a live data element able to be manipulated by the reader. With an interactive table, one can choose to sort data within columns, can rearrange columns, and can conceivably perform mathematic operations with the data, treating the table like a live spreadsheet. It is likely that readers will have questions that the author did not think to ask, and providing the data in this interactive way can help readers ask and answer queries independent of the author's commentary on the static table.

Dealing with data than cannot be manipulated in a tabular format is not enough. To be a truly useful, living archaeological publication, its tables need to become four-dimensional, introducing the time element. Archaeology is notoriously messy and inexact, and our publications do their best to make sense of the mess. It is likely that some material gets left out of a publication for whatever reason, or in the case of some excavations, material (e.g., lamps, coins, etc.) that is assigned only covers a range of years from that excavation. Any material excavated after the time period assigned to one researcher is dumped into a future publication. With an online "monograph," newly recovered material (or material from years after an original assignment) can be added to the data set from which our interactive tables produce information for the reader. By allowing a publication to remain open, new data can be entered upon discovery.

These kinds of on-the-fly edits make it difficult to identify the "version of record," that version which is cited by other scholars when completing their own research. I propose that we follow the model used in wikis where a date/time-stamp and author ID are assigned whenever a page changes, and that the researchers citing that page include the date when that page was accessed. If that is too extreme, then perhaps the software model can be followed wherein iterations (updates) are assigned incremental numbers whenever something changes in the code.

Maps

Maps work perfectly well in two-dimensional, print publications, but being able to bring them online in 3D is a necessity, especially when trying to understand the topography of a settlement, city, or region. By visualizing the geographic setting, both authors and readers can begin to draw conclusions about the placement of settlements (or structures within them), and how they relate to natural features in the landscape. Authors can also choose to indicate on maps where artifacts were recovered, where features like graves, pits, wells, etc., are located, all on a sliding scale for granularity depending on the kind of access granted to the reader. It is possible that sensitive data such as findspots can be abused, so it may be that some level of security will need to be supplied to on-screen readers, or more simply, the excavation, its authors, and the publisher exercise common sense in determining how fine a grain is necessary for most readers while giving them the option to contact the excavation for permission to access higher resolution map data.

While 3D maps are crucial to archaeological publications, again, adding the element of time to online maps should be required. Some sites existed for periods of months or years, while others spanned decades, centuries, and millennia. For those sites that have experienced long periods of occupation, their maps should include a "timeline slider." Readers can use the slider to watch the site change dynamically from decade to decade, period to period. Stopping time on the map, one can then observe features, and could conceivably tap or click on those to drill down to more information. As excavation proceeds and more data are collected and published, these maps will change automatically, including the new data input by the excavators over the course of a season. 3D maps are important and provide a snapshot of a site or region in time, but making the maps temporally dynamic can provide maximum use for readers and they consider new questions or conceive new hypotheses based on their observations of the maps and the data they provide.

Images

Traditional, two-dimensional drawings are extraordinarily useful when communicating the profile of a potsherd, of the preserved letter forms in an inscription in stone, and designs and decorations, among other things. Print publications make frequent use of these, complementing the black-and-white drawings with black-and-white photos (aka "halftones") that provide additional visual data of excavations and their artifacts either as they are, or as they were. Printing in color is expensive, and archaeologists are often charged by their publishers should they wish to have some "art" appear in color for their article or book. It would seem that economics has had an adverse effect on imaging archaeology in print, preventing color from being used when it might have provided additional (or different) data not communicated from an image in grayscale. Online publication completely removes economics from the decision-making process of choosing whether something should be illustrated in color or not.

I defer to the other contributors of this volume to write about 3D archaeology and imaging to write about how they use it and the technologies employed to create 3D maps, scans, reproductions, etc. It should be obvious to the reader that a 3D scan of an artifact provides information that a two-dimensional drawing or photograph cannot. There are Open Source utilities now available that can rotate two-dimensional pottery profiles, creating a 3D image to allow the reader to fully visualize what pottery, lamps, etc., would have looked like in the round. The problem remains that even with 3D views and reconstructions, they are still viewed through two-dimensional media: screens. This is not unlike printing a 3D image in a book, although at least with online 3D imagery, one can pan/zoom/rotate.

I propose that for 3D images to be truly useful to the reader, that they be printed using 3D printers (see Olson et al. in this volume), based on printer specs provided to the reader by the author/publisher. Imagine printing your own set of plates, or printing bones/fragments, or even a scale model of a house or temple. Traditional photography and drawing work well when providing their data via traditional, two-dimensional media. 3D imaging, to be most useful, should require either 3D printing, or the use of glasses or headgear such as Oculus Rift (http://www.oculusvr.com/) to provide an immersive 3D experience.

As for four-dimensional aspects of imaging, it is possible to include the time element when looking at a site over a period of years as it has undergone excavation, or in some cases, how a city has grown around an ancient monument. For 3D reconstructions, a time slider could be used to view reconstructions of buildings or settlements throughout different periods. There are likely other applications that I am missing, but I suspect others have already posed this question and come up with answers.

With digital imaging in electronic publications, there is one major issue that must be considered: scale. In a print monograph, the publisher sizes an image on the page and then prints the scale of the object in the image caption. Some publishers opt to include scale bars in their images, while others crop the scale bar out, relying on the caption to tell the reader what the size of the object pictured is. Because the printed page is static, the image size never changes. On e-readers, however (including smartphones, tablets, laptops, desktop computers, etc.), the "page" and the image are resized constantly. Printing the scale in a caption does not help, and leaving the scale bar in the image approaches the ridiculous as either tiny or large depending on how the reader resizes a drawing or photo. It may be possible to create a widget that dynamically changes the scale of the image based on its relative size on a screen. As a reader increases an image's size for a better look at a detail, the scale would change from 1:3 to 3:1. Until that happens (unless it already has), readers might have to go on the measurements of an imaged artifact that are printed in the body or catalogue text and then eyeball the image to guestimate its actual size.

One potentially unexpected barrier to publishing archaeological material fully (and freely) online is that of image permissions. Countries such as Greece and Turkey have yet to update their guidelines for image permissions to include the current state of digital and online publication, especially for scholarly purposes. Greece's Archaeological Receipts Fund (TAP) currently defines an electronic publication as a webpage and makes no provision for e-books or other kinds of digital media. It is either a website or it is not, and if it is, you can have permission to post that image for a maximum of three years before Greece, as the rights-holder of any image taken of any monument/artifact in-country, requires you to take it down. On the form to request permission from Greece to publish an image of a monument or artifact via digital media is language stating to the effect that it might take months for the bureaucracy to consider the application at which point it could either be rejected or a permissions fee assessed. There is little hope in Greece's current state that this issue will be addressed; it is the least of that country's worries.

Conclusion

Archaeology is messy, and it deals with 3D artifacts in four-dimensional space-time. Its publications should reflect that. At our current level of technology, it is possible to create archaeological publications in an open, online environment that incorporates text, 2D and 3D imagery, interactive 2D and 3D maps, and interactive data sets, and omni-directional links to content and context managed by others. Our new publications must incorporate all of these elements to create a record and interpretation of what we have discovered, leaving that data and interpretation open to criticism, dialogue, and growth over time. Universities, archaeological field schools, and publishers need to make a concerted effort to educate archaeologists to the potential provided by new media and existing technology as it can serve to document work done. The editor's role should be to apply standards and style, to fact check, to clean up inconsistencies, to verify and standardize notes and bibliography, at which point it can be published, handed over to the crowd for the necessary – but until now missing – step of post-publication peer review.

Practice

6.
Closing Gaps with Low-Cost 3D

Sebastian Heath

Introduction

I start with a personal statement: I use 3D tools because I want to bridge the gap between my work in the field—which is mainly with Roman objects, particularly ceramics—and anyone who might be interested in my efforts. To put that another way, I am able to experience objects and sites directly and I want to share the best approximation of my own access with others. "Access" is the key word here. For me, that is what 3D modeling is all about.

Optimism and Context

I will also begin by saying I am an optimist and think that the recent drop in the cost of generating models and the current opportunities for free distribution of those models mean that change is in the air. Of course, 3D technologies have been available for many years so it is important to stress that there are pioneering archaeologists who dove in well before I did. And I note that they have done so in ways that have made substantive contributions to our understanding of major issues in Mediterranean archaeology. The Stanford Digital Forma Urbis Romae Project (Levoy and Trimble n.d.) (http://formaurbis.stanford.edu), as well as (Frischer 2013) obviously merit mention here (http://romereborn.frischerconsulting.com); as does Philip Sapirstein's (2010–2011) ACLS-funded online publication of 3D models from Mons Repos at Corfu (http://sites.museum.upenn.edu/monrepos/). This project is distinguished by making its data available for download under a Creative Commons license. And I also briefly note work in Emerita Augusta, modern Merida in Spain, that has helped confirm and improve the re-assembly of non-joining statue fragments from the so-called "Marble Forum" in the heart of the Roman colony into a convincing Aeneas, Anchises, Ascanius group (Mercan et al. 2011). These models give vivid context to A. Jiménez's more theoretical discussion of "mimesis" in Roman Hispania, in which that group receives considerable attention (Jiménez 2010).

Longer-term History

But having noted pre-existing work, I think it is worth recognizing that in the history of technology, origins and early efforts are not inherently more interesting than phases of rapid adoption. As Olson and Placchetti (in this volume) describe, new tools are making it easier for more archaeologists to use 3D techniques. To offer a personal perspective, my own first attempts at making models using photo-based reconstruction were entirely the result of recognizing in the fall of 2012 that costs had become low, that ease of use had improved, and that distribution was possible using well-known standards (as in, "No Plug-ins!"). These three factors in combination meant there was no longer good reason not to integrate 3D into my own work as an archaeologist. And I should emphasize that it has been enjoyable to follow colleagues on Twitter who have come to the same conclusion. Again, change is in the air.

But before showing the current state of my efforts, I would like to establish a long-term historical, or perhaps historiographic, perspective. Figure 1 shows Plate 34 from the report on the 1881 American excavations at Assos (Clarke et al. 1882), the text of which is available for download from the Hathi Trust Digital Library. The dominant mode of representation of this Roman sarchophagus is linear, but shadow is used to bring out the relatively deep relief of the bucrania and the drooping garlands. Such shadows are a convention that has fallen out of favor in contemporary technical illustration. The same is true for the female figure seated at the right of the sarcophagus. There is much to say about her, and she is an evocative intermediary between the object being represented and viewers of this image. To the extent that there is tension between the precise metric scale below the sarcophagus and our female guide, the "clinical" won that tug-of-war with the "perceptual." Meaning that in more modern illustrations such human figures are part of recreations and are less welcome in technical and measured drawings.

This trend from realism to abstraction is particularly apparent in current best practices for the illustration of wheel-made ceramic vessels. Figure 2 shows a drawing by Piet de Jong of a late Roman table vessel (an African Red-Slip Hayes form 97 of the 6th century A.D. to be more specific) as viewable on the website of the Athenian Agora Excavations. It is a representation that emphasizes shape, depth, surface treatment, and color all in one image. As a recent catalog of de Jong's Agora illustrations noted of this drawing, "his watercolor is a peek into all aspects of the pot" (Papadopoulos 2006: no. 129). Now compare it with figure 3, a profile drawing of an ARS form 87 found at Troy (Heath and Tekkok n.d.: P18.0093:1; http://classics.uc.edu/troy/grbpottery/html/ars.html). Such profile drawings are the "gold standard" of modern ceramic publication. When well-executed, they permit a ceramicist to confidently compare an example in-hand to a drawing of a potentially similar piece. That is an important step in the full analysis of a ceramic assemblage. But it is also important to note that there is nothing "realistic" about profile drawings. They utilize a code of sorts that requires considerable mental processing to move from their abstract representation to a sense of the real vessel.

The above was a very long way of saying that we are catching up with—and going beyond—where we have always wanted to be. That is another "gap" potentially closed.

Models at Kenchreai

As for my own work, three models will show that I am in the early stages of closing gaps between what I am doing in the field and my stated goal of sharing as much as I can. Figures 4, 5, and 6 are screen captures that link to the site "p3d.in," one of a few options for sharing 3D models that are currently available. All of them come from my work as part of the American Excavations at Kenchreai, which operates with a permit from the Greek Ministry of Culture and under the auspices of the American School of Classical Studies at Athens. I am very grateful to the project director Joseph Rife of Vanderbilt University for the opportunity to include these models in this discussion.

The first model (Fig. 4) is of a Late Roman lamp (KE 235). A brief description of creating it is online via a guest post I contributed to John Wallrodt's Paperless Archaeology blog (Heath 2013; http://paperlessarchaeology.com/2013/08/14/two-kenchreai-3d-models/). Its original inventory information is available as part of the Kenchreai Archaeological Archive (http://kenchreai.github.io/kaa/KE0235).

My second model (Fig. 5) is a statue base with figure preserved only to just above the ankles (KE 1221). It is a beautiful piece and I hope that even this preliminary model captures some its interest. Its preliminary documentation is also available online (http://kenchreai.github.io/kaa/KE1221).

The third model (Fig. 6) is of a stretch of marble stylobate from the so-called "Aphrodiseion" at Kenchreai (Scranton et al. 1978, p. 79).

As noted, the three images below are screen captures from the model sharing website P3D.in and readers can click on the associated links to go directly to the relevant page there. Assuming you are using a compatible browser—Safari, Chrome, or FireFox, but not Internet Explorer—it should be possible to rotate and zoom in on the models.

That access is the illustration of my opening point and the current fulfillment of the title of this post. By which I mean that even within the context of a relatively small project that needs to be careful with its resources, the creation of 3D models is possible. And not just creation, but sharing as well. That is "gap" closing.

A next step is re-use. I illustrate that by way of a fanciful combination of scaled versions of my three example models (Fig. 7). The dataset is too big to load usefully into p3d.in so the image is static, but I hope that it hints at a future in which ready availability of 3D data closes gaps between categories of object, their original contexts, and the archaeological (or other) sub-disciplines that study them.

One final point: it should be clear that this is all work in progress. The models are far from perfect and my colleagues at Kenchreai and I are in the early stages of thinking about how new opportunities can contribute to our research design. One sign that the project considers these models "final" will be that end users can download them and do their own mixing, or to put that differently, their own research. That will not be quite the same as being on site or handling the lamp and statue in-person. But it should be clear that I am optimistic that this access will be close enough to enable new "peeks" at aspects of the material that were previously available only to a very few.

Works Cited

Clarke, J. T., W. C. Lawton, and J. S. Diller. 1882. *Report on the investigations at Assos, 1881.* Boston: A. Williams.

Frischer, B. 2013. *Rome Reborn.* http://romereborn.frischerconsulting.com.

Heath, S. 2013-08-14. "Two Kenchreai 3D models," *Paperless Archaeology* http://paperlessarchaeology.com/2013/08/14/two-kenchreai-3d-models/.

Heath, S.. and B. Tekkök. n.d.. "African Red Slip," in *Greek, Roman and Byzantine Pottery at Ilion.* http://classics.uc.edu/troy/grbpottery/html/ars.html.

Jiménez, A. 2010. "Reproducing Difference: Mimesis and Colonialism in Roman Hispania," in B. Knapp and P. van Dommelen, eds., *Material Connections: Mobility, Materiality and Mediterranean Identities.* Abingdon, Oxon: Routledge, 38–63.

Levoy, M., and J. Trimble. n.d. *Stanford Digital Forma Urbis Romae Project.* http://formaurbis.stanford.edu.

Merchán, P., S. Salamanca, and A. Adán. 2011. "Restitution of Sculptural Groups Using 3D Scanners," *Sensors* 11: 8497–8518.

Papadopoulos, J. K., J. M. K. Camp, and J. P. De. 2007. *The Art of Antiquity: Piet de Jong and the Athenian Agora.* Princeton: American School of Classical Studies at Athens.

Sapirstein, P. (2010 – 2011). *The Archaic Sanctuary of Mons Repos at Corfu.* http://sites.museum.upenn.edu/monrepos/.

Scranton, R. L., J. W. Shaw, and L. Ibrahim. 1978. *Kenchreai Eastern Port of Corinth: I, Topography and Architecture.* Leiden: Brill.

PLATE 34. SARCOPHAGUS, RESTORED.

Figure 1: Plate 34 from Clarke et al. 1882, as available via hathitrust.org

Figure 2: African Red Slip Hayes form 97 (Agora P 9656) as illustrated by Piet de Jong. Reproduced by permission of American School of Classical Studies, Agora Excavations

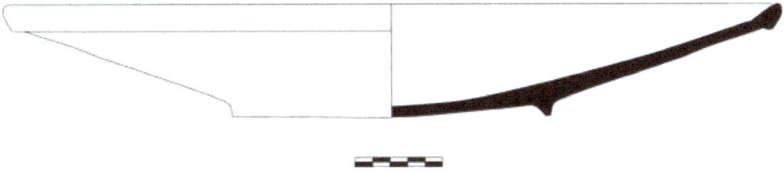

Figure 3: African Red Slip Hayes form 87 as illustrated by the Troy Excavations. Reproduced by permission.

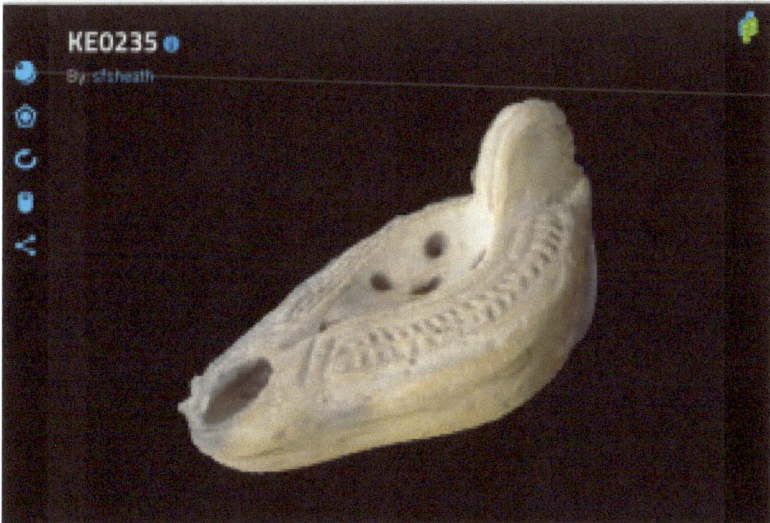

Figure 4: 3D model of inventoried object KE 235 (Late Roman lamp) displayed in p3d.in. Reproduced by permission of American Excavations at Kenchreai.

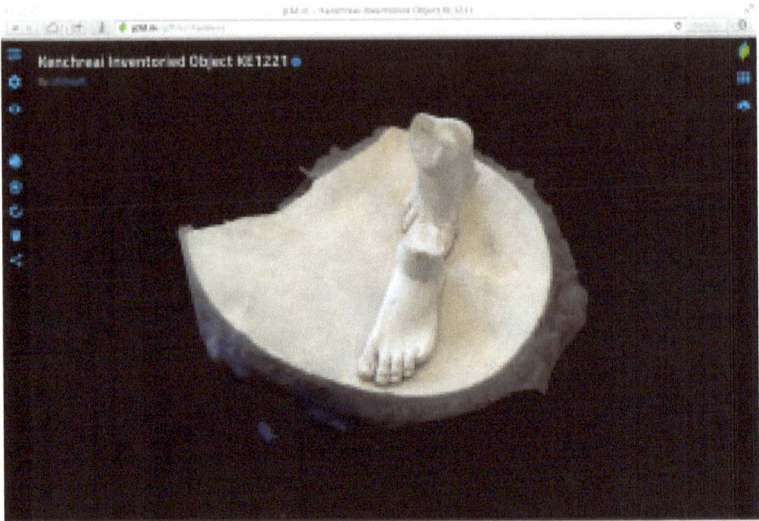

Figure 5: 3D model of inventoried object KE 1221 (Roman statue base) displayed in p3d.in. Reproduced by permission of American Excavations at Kenchreai.

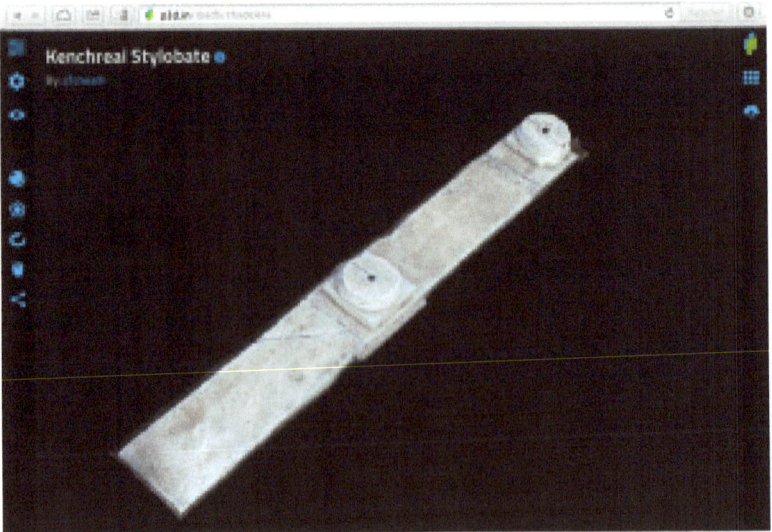

Figure 6: 3D model of *in situ* architecture from Kenchreai displayed in p3d.in. Reproduced by permission of American Excavations at Kenchreai.

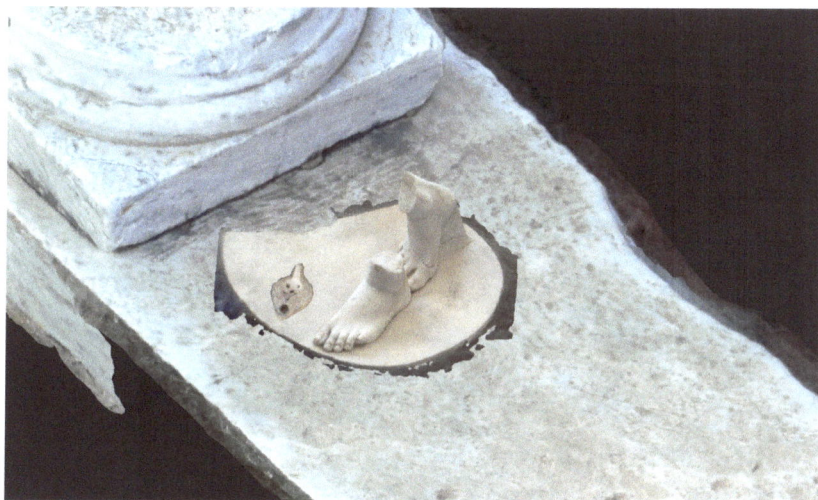

Figure 7: "fanciful combination"of figs. 5 and 6. Reproduced by permission of American Excavations at
Kenchreai.

7.
3D Models as Analytical Tools

Ethan Gruber

Introduction

Several years ago, when I was still a graduate student at the University of Virginia, I took part in a sort of digital humanities speed dating event hosted by the Scholars' Lab (http://scholarslab.org), for whom I was employed as a web developer at the time. This event was geared toward creating connections between technologists and humanists at the university. I remember a brief encounter with two archaeologists in the anthropology department (a department separate from my own classical archaeology program, which was part of the art history department) who saw only dubious benefit of 3D within the discipline. Models were seen by my colleagues as more of a sexy technological endeavor with little or no scholarly application. I discussed with them some of my own work in lighting simulation of 3D reconstructions, similar to the work recently undertaken by Bernie Frischer and John Fillwalk on the solar interaction between the Horologium Augusti and the Ara Pacis (http://www.heritagedaily.com/2014/01/ball-state-simulation-helps-unravel-ancient-roman-puzzle/100629), and so I hoped they developed a greater respect for the technology after enhancing their understanding of it.

We have seen in previous contributions to this volume the value of 3D models in archaeological documentation and pedagogy, and so I wanted to discuss the value of architectural models as scholarly tools, enabling us to visualize the built environment and test hypotheses in ways that were previously impossible. My aim here is not necessarily to detail the results of these simulations (since you can find open access papers about most of these projects), but rather the provide a synopsis of the thought processes that go into creating the reconstructions and the evolution of my own sunlight simulation methodology, which has grown more sophisticated over the years.

The House of the Faun

My first foray into lighting simulation was purely accidental. In 2008, I used Autodesk Maya to create a 3D model of Pompeii's House of the Faun, one of the largest and best known houses in the city (http://www.autodesk.com/products/autodesk-maya/overview). The model was created for a graduate seminar taught by John Dobbins to test hypothetical sight lines in a typical Italian atrium house. Sight lines are often presumed to be an integral part of Roman architecture. Architectural historians quite often depend on 2D plans to formulate their hypotheses. In theory, the open doors of the atrium house would invite passersby to gaze inside, revealing an architectural and social hierarchy of sorts: one may see the gardens beyond the tablinum, but may only enter this space if he or she is of higher social status and invited by the paterfamilias into this more intimate environment. The House of the Faun is a more special case, for just beyond the peristyle is the exedra containing the famous mosaic of Alexander the Great, and beyond this is yet another, larger peristylen (Fig. 1). As it turns out, the sight line analysis of the 3D model of the house reveals that it is basically impossible to see the exedra from the street, when basing the model upon the standard reconstructions found in printed illustrations.

Near the end of the semester, I happened upon a Maya script written by a lecturer of architecture at TU Delft, Thijs Welman, which allows a user to input the latitude and longitude of the structure, as well as the precise minute in time (back to 2000 B.C.), in order to accurately set the model's sunlight angle. Once the angle is set, the model can be rendered with physically accurate light and shadows. I corresponded with Welman briefly several years ago and he was surprised that his script had found its way into the hands of an archaeologist—it had merely been intended to accurately render sunlight in the models of architecture students. He even extended the script, by my request, to animate the sunlight entity in Maya, enabling the rendering of time-lapse videos.

I proceeded to render the exedra and the mosaic contained within on the equinoxes and solstices of 100 B.C., the approximate date of the mosaic's installation. In the summertime, the angle of the sun was high enough that the mosaic was completely enshrouded in shadow. In the winter, however, the low sun projected six long shadows across the mosaic, certainly not an ideal viewing condition (Fig. 2).

When John Dobbins and I went to Pompeii the following summer (2009), we went into the House of the Faun and began to take note of peculiar architectural features, which ultimately led us to conclude that when the new Roman overlords colonized Pompeii following the Social Wars, the Roman patron of the house planned serious renovations of the peristyle, installed the exedra, the Alexander mosaic, and removed several columns and part of the portico to enhance the experience of encountering the space (Fig. 3). For further details, please see our paper, presented at CAA in 2010 (Gruber and Dobbins 2013b). Time-lapse videos are available for both the summer and winter solstices (Summer solstice: https://vimeo. com/83737609 and Winter solstice: https://vimeo.com/83737610).

The House of the Drinking Contest

In 2009, I began working on a reconstruction of the House of the Drinking Contest, a late Severan period house in Seleucia Pieria, the port city of Antioch (Gruber and Dobbins 2013a). There were two purposes for this model: to test the sight line hypothesis proposed by Dobbins (Dobbins 2000) and to import images of the house's elaborate mosaics into the model and apply the lighting simulation methodology first tested on the House of the Faun to recontextualize the artworks in order to experience them in the same environment that the ancient inhabitants of the house once (theoretically) experienced them. It was during this project that I began delving more deeply in the technological and theoretical aspects of the simulations and found that these methodologies had been applied first in Simon Ellis (1994) and in subsequent publications (Ellis 2000, 2007). Ellis' methodology has been tremendously influential on my own scholarship, as he is one of the true pioneers in the adaptation of 3D models to archaeological research. The conclusions that he reached in his houses were quite similar to my own in the House of the Drinking Contest: that the setting sun in the spring and summer months shone through large doors of the triclinium, illuminating a grand central mosaic (Fig. 4). It is at this moment that guests would gather near the patron to take part in the symposium, with the most brilliant work of art illuminated with its glass and polished stone tesserae visible to all in a way that would otherwise never be visible earlier in the day or other times of year.

With respect to sight lines, Dobbins hypothesized that irregular inter-columniations within the colonnade bordering on the north side of the courtyard allowed for direct views from rooms on the north side of the house to the south (Fig. 5). But what lay south? The archival photographs from the 1930s provide some glimpse, but by some stroke of luck, I was able to find a georeferenced photograph in Panoramio (discovered through Google Earth) of the same viewpoint taken from within 100 or 200 hundred meters from the site. Incorporating this photo into the model, I was able to simulate this hypothetical view through picture windows, glancing toward the shoreline of the Mediterranean and Mount Casius beyond (Fig. 6). I have subsequently found a plethora of archaeological and literary examples of views to mountains and seas (and the legal protection of scenic views and sunlight in the domestic sphere), particularly from the Roman East during the Late Antique period (Lippolis 2007). But in archaeology, as we know, context is everything. How exactly do we know that there was not a structure directly south of this house blocking this view? We do not know for certain, but we can be reasonably sure this was not the case, based on the topography. The House of the Drinking Contest and those houses built to the east and west were built on a terrace—the land sloped downward to the south, toward the sea. So while there may have been more houses to the south, they would have been lower to sea level, and therefore unlikely to have obstructed the view from this house. I believe this is an important point to drive home to anyone modeling reconstructions for scholarly purposes: artifacts must be placed back into context within the architecture, but one needs to take into consideration the larger topography surrounding the architecture. How do the walls and roofs affect the illumination of the mosaics? How does the natural or urban environment interact with the house itself?

The Temple of Artemis at Ephesus

The final test case for 3D as a platform for scholarly analysis I would like to briefly discuss a reconstruction of the Temple of Artemis at Ephesus. I modeled this in a graduate seminar on Anatolian archaeology to determine whether one could view the epiphany of Artemis from within the temple: a sight line from the central pedimental window, toward and above the rear wall of the altar, to the cult statue below (Fig. 7).

While this may have been possible in the Archaic temple built by Croesus in 550 B.C., it would not have been possible in the 4th-century temple, based on archaeological measurements (Fig. 8). I applied the sunlight simulation methodology to observe the temple at different times of day throughout the year, but nothing particularly notable stood out. Unlike in the House of the Faun, where only the walls and roofs of the house affect the lighting within it, a structure of the size of this temple is largely unaffected by the built environment surrounding it. There was, however, potential for the physical topography to affect the lighting of the temple. The Austrian Archaeological Institute was gracious enough to provide me with their 10-meter resolution Digital Elevation Model for Ephesus. To the southwest of the temple (between the temple and the Hellenistic/Roman city) lay the mountain, Panayirda. It was necessary to observe the interaction between this mountain and the sunlight and in the waning hours on the winter solstice, shadows cast by the mountain fell upon the temple. It is not apparent that the architects of the temple took into deliberate consideration the sun's effect on the structure, unlike those who designed the Augustan monuments in the Campus Martius.

Conclusions

3D models and simulations have enormous potential in furthering archaeological scholarship. They enable us to test hypotheses that could otherwise never have been examined, to observe the environmental conditions and context in which artworks and artifacts were placed in their own time, and, furthermore, formulate ideas that would never have been imagined by our predecessors before the digital age. The House of the Faun is an example of this, I think. Simulations within the 3D reconstruction altered our perception of the ruins and the next time we visited them, and we developed a different interpretation of the evidence. The final issue that must be noted is that everything discussed above is somewhat theoretical. While sunlight angles themselves are grounded in mathematical fact, reconstructions of ancient architecture are inherently theoretical. We create models that are plausible, based on data we have available, but these data are often incomplete or confusing. Thus, the simulations are not absolute truth, but rather a potential explanation of the past. The flexibility of 3D models allows us to address alternative scenarios based on new evidence or interpretations.

68

Works Cited

Dobbins, J. 2000. "The Houses of Antioch," in C. Kondoleon, ed., *Antioch: The Lost Ancient City.* Princeton: Princeton University Press, pp 51-62.

Ellis, S. 1994. "Lighting in Late Roman Houses," in S. Cottam, D. Dungworth, S. Scott, and J. Taylor, eds., *TRAC 94: Proceedings of the Fourth Annual Theoretical Roman Archaeology Conference, Durham 1994.* Oxford: Oxbow Books, 65–71.

Ellis, S. 2000. *Roman Housing.* London: Duckworth.

Ellis, S. 2007. "Shedding Light on Late Roman Housing," in L. Lavan, L. Özgenel, A. C. Sarantis, eds., *Housing in Late Antiquity: From Palaces to Shops.* Leiden: Brill, 283–302.

Gruber, E., and J. Dobbins. 2013a. "Illuminating Historical Architecture: The House of the Drinking Contest at Antioch," in F. Contreras, M. Farjas, and F. J. Melero, *Fusion of Cultures. Proceedings of the 38th Annual Conference on Computer Application and Quantitative Methods in Archaeology, Granada, Spain, April 2010.* BAR International Series 2494. Oxford: B.A.R., pp. 71-76.

Gruber, E., and J. Dobbins. 2013b. "Modeling Hypotheses in Pompeian Archaeology: The House of the Faun," in F. Contreras, M. Farjas, and F. J. Melero, *Fusion of Cultures. Proceedings of the 38th Annual Conference on Computer Application and Quantitative Methods in Archaeology, Granada, Spain, April 2010.* BAR International Series 2494. Oxford: B.A.R., pp. 77-84.

Lippolis, I. B. 2007. "Private Space in Late Antique Cities," in L. Lavan, L. Özgenel, A. C. Sarantis, eds., *Housing in Late Antiquity: From Palaces to Shops.* Leiden: Brill, 197–237.

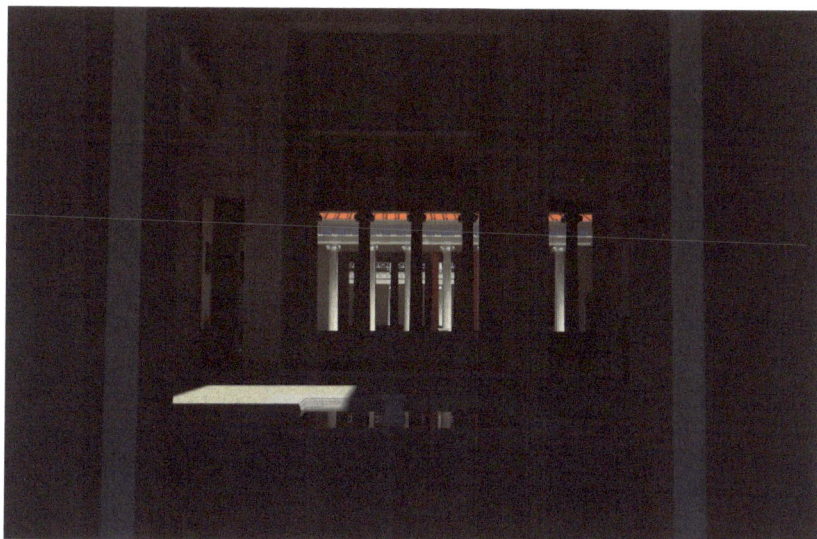

Figure 1: View from the fauces to the Alexander exedra in the House of the Faun.

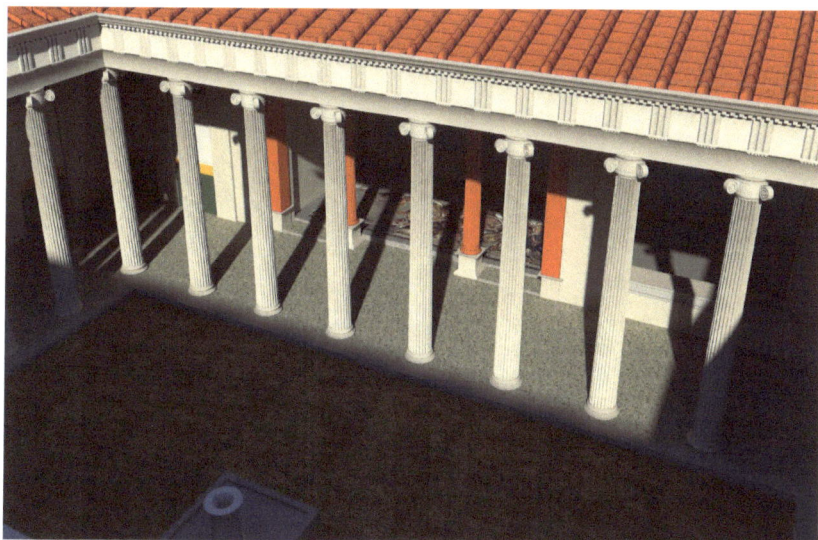

Figure 2: About noon, December 21, 100 B.C.:
commonly accepted reconstruction.

Figure 3: About noon, December 21, 100 B.C.:
alternate reconstruction.

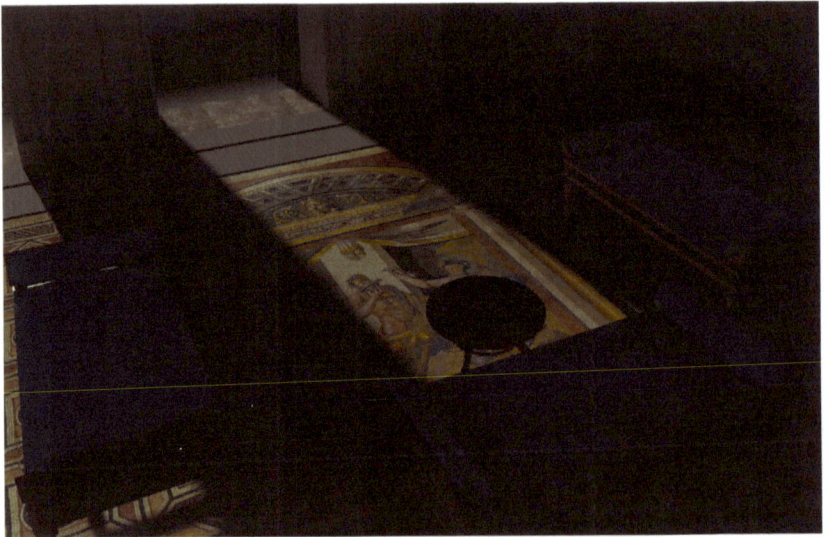

Figure 4: Triclinium: June 21, A.D. 230, 6pm.

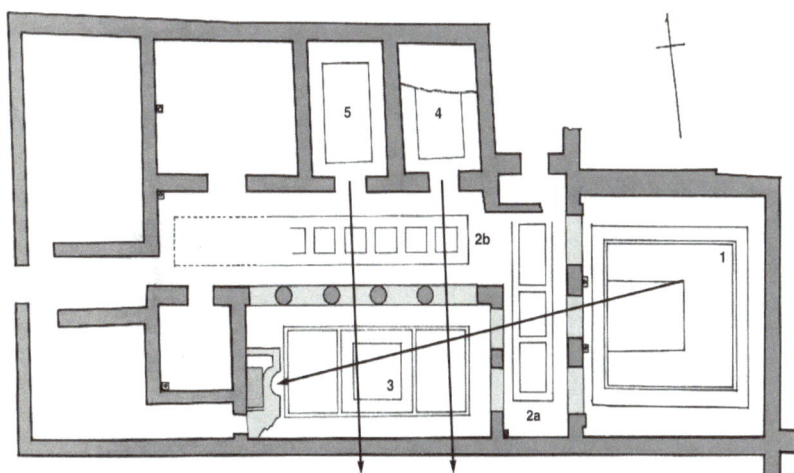

Figure 5: Plan of the House of the
Drinking Contest.

Figure 6: View toward the sea and
Mount Casius to the south.

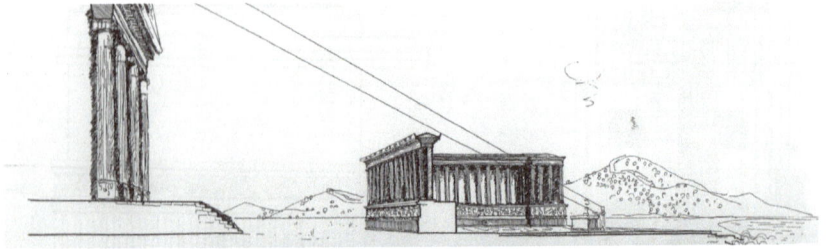

Figure 7: Witnessing the epiphany of Artemis from
the pedimental windows.

Figure 8: Hypothesis applied to the
reconstruction.

8.
Three Dimensional Field Recording in Archaeology:
An Example from Gabii

Rachel Opitz

Introduction

In asking for contributions to this series of posts reflecting on 3D modeling in archaeology, Bill Caraher posed a series of questions, one of which was:

"What is the future of 3D modeling in archaeology? At present, the 3D image is useful for illustrating artifacts and - in some cases - presenting archaeological and architectural relationships, but it has yet to prove itself as an essential basis for analysis or as a robust medium for communicating robust archaeological description. Will 3D visualization become more than just another method for providing illustrations for archaeological arguments?"

I'd very much like to answer "yes" to the question posed above. I'm going to argue that 3D modeling and visualizations can be the grounds for the re-interpretation of a type of essential archaeological evidence, stratigraphic sequences, in a way that goes beyond just providing illustrations for arguments and conclusions drawn from other evidence. To make this argument, I'll start by providing a bit of background about 3D field recording at Gabii - an irreverent history of our digital documentation method and how it evolved.

3D at Gabii

In 2009 Prof. Nicola Terrenato, with the enthusiasm and support of the Project's other directors, decided to open a fairly large excavation area at Gabii. Among the Project's priorities was the development of a field survey method that would let us work quickly, so we could make efficient progress excavating in a big urban area. This would allow us to ask and maybe answer some big questions like 'How did the urban fabric develop, change over time, and decay at Gabii?' In addition to a fast survey-to-GIS-to-printed plan strategy, as an experiment, we were going to try recording some of the more complex contexts using photomodeling, as we called it after the Eos PhotoModeler software. Photomodeling would allow us to rapidly produce orthophotos of complex contexts, thereby avoiding tedious stone by stone survey in the field (Fig. 1).

Luckily in 2009 we didn't find much in the way of complex architecture or stratigraphy. We modeled a few contexts in the course of the season, and they turned out well. We were confident enough in the technique's efficacy that when an orientalizing infant burial was uncovered on the last day on site (see Becker and Nowlin, 2011) 3D modeling was our primary means of recording the remains, and we were only a little nervous (Fig. 2). In 2010, when we started uncovering an Imperial necropolis and the remains of two houses, we used Photomodeling (more formally known as Structure From Motion (SFM), or Image Based Modeling (IBM), or Digital Close Range Photogrammetry (DCRP)) to record all the structural and human remains. Photomodeling swiftly, and as the result of a conscious decision to fully implement a new approach to the site's documentation, transitioned from being an experiment to being a key part of our recording strategy. In 2011 the scale of the excavation grew considerably. As a result of this rapid expansion were left with a substantial backlog for model processing at the end of the field season. The need to undertake substantial amounts of post-season processing was obviously undesirable. Photomodeling was intended to speed up and facilitate the excavation and documentation process, and not add to the delays in producing documentation ready for interpretation and write-ups which are typical of all too many excavation projects. Post-season research in 2011 led us to switch to Agisoft Photoscan for the 2012 field season. The faster processing times and ability to batch script in python helped us to complete the 2011 field season's documentation in one season and get back on top of the workflow. 2012 was also the year that we introduced Unity3D on site as a tool for building and sharing more complex scenes showing 3D models of multiple contexts. This browser based approach to sharing was considered an improvement over the use of Meshlab or ArcGIS, both of which, while fundamentally simple to use, require download and install of software, a step that could be viewed as an obstacle.

2012 was also the year that we switched to LP Archaeology's ARK system for our descriptive data management (http://ark.lparchaeology.com/) This was a fortuitous convergence, as having a web-based data management system meant that linking from the Unity3D content and from GIS content to database entries was fairly simple. Some 2012 post-season work was devoted to promoting ARK and Unity3D within the group as a means of distributing and presenting the models. Notably, several members of the excavation staff kindly agreed to participate in an interpretive experiment, which I discuss below. All of this was good news, because 2013 brought us the largest, most complex collection of structural remains to date. We finished the season with a small, but manageable backlog.

In short, the field recording system fundamentally works, six hundred odd individual models later. We've gone from SFM as an experiment to SFM as normal. I think this is one of the more important things we can say about 3D field recording at Gabii. It's just part of the routine - a proven method (Fig. 3).

All of the excavators feel that the interpretive sketch is still essential (a point on which we are entirely in agreement) and sometimes worry that all the excitement surrounding SFM and the speed it encourages us to document at will end up de-emphasizing actually looking at the archaeology, reflecting on what you see, and interpreting it via drawing carefully and slowly. This is an important ongoing debate about field recording within the team. The technology encourages us to speed up so we can work at larger scales, an important shift, as we've said, that permits us to ask and attempt to respond to large-scale questions, but the archaeology usually demands that we slow down and think about what we're doing. The integration of digital technologies and 'close range remote sensing' into the daily excavation routine therefore represents a constant balancing and re-balancing of practice, speeding up where we can and slowing down when needed. It takes discipline on the part of the entire excavation team to not drift into a false sense of security based on the seeming completeness of SFM models. To their credit, area supervisors and excavators actively promote conscientious documentation and remain on guard against letting the technology overtake careful documentation and thinking and interpretation in the field. I don't expect this particular conversation to end any time soon, nor would I want it to end, as I think this kind of constant monitoring of the balance between speed and detail, between rapid documentation of basic data and taking the time to make thoughtful interpretations is good field archaeology.

Five years in, we're still adapting our approach as the nature of the archaeology we are encountering changes, but for us most of the debate has moved from 3D recording as a field method to the implications of the 3D documentation for publication, communication and interpretation. I've taken a not inconsiderable amount of space to talk about the development of our field recording system because I think in order to talk about the question which Bill posed, about the role of 3D modeling beyond illustration, as part of analysis or as a robust communication medium, it has to be everywhere, fully integrated into the normal recording practice of an excavation. If it's something being done experimentally, for only a few contexts, or in a limited area, if it's not part of the excavator's practice, then it really can't be fully part of the interpretive stage or the communication and publication stage. Equally, it can't just be in the hands of the project's specialists. It has to be used by the project's team at large (something only starting to happen for us now). The length of the narrative above reflects the incremental way in which new technologies and practices develop and become part of excavation methodology, something that happens through a sustained effort over an extended period.

Critically Evaluating Digital Data via Peer Review

In 2013 we embarked on an NEH funded project, *21st c. Data, 21st c. Publications: 3D Data and Building the Peer Reviewer Community*, in which we are trying to use 3D content as more than a tool for documentation (m-gabii. adsroot.itcs.umich.edu/gabiigoesdigital). This project focuses on developing a process for the peer reviewed publication of the kinds of digital 3D models and complex, interactive datasets that projects like ours are now producing using SFM and related 3D field recording technologies, and building a community of peer reviewers with a shared frame of reference for evaluating these publications. This project is bringing us, at last, close to engaging with Bill's question, "Will 3D visualization become more than just another method for providing illustrations for archaeological arguments? [Can 3D modeling] prove itself as an essential basis for analysis or as a robust medium for communicating robust archaeological description? " The peer review process is designed to, among other things, help authors strengthen their argument and clarify its presentation. As researchers and academics, we're trained to recognize good and bad writing, and to identify holes and weaknesses in a argument. We learn what makes a useful chart or illustration. But what does good, useful interactive 3D content look like?

What are the qualities on which it should be assessed? To develop a framework for the critique and review of what is essentially mixed visual and written content, we have to think about the link between visualization and interpretation and ask ourselves: Is visualization illustration, or part of the interpretive process and a means of interrogating the data? This question represents, I think, the nub of Bill's broader question about illustration, description and archaeological argument. In responding to this question, I would argue that these models should be understood in the context of the discipline of information visualization, as part of a school of visual communication and argument ranging from John Tukey's writing on *Exploratory Data Analysis* (1977) through Nathan Yau's posts on flowingdata.com.

This perspective no doubt stems from my work as an archaeologist away from the Gabii Project, in which I specialize in airborne laserscanning (ALS) applications in archaeology, a field in which information visualization and visual interpretation are viewed as fundamental parts of the research process. Consequently, I'm predisposed to think that creating and engaging with visualizations is part of the process of interpretation, and necessary to understanding the physical remains 'on the ground' and the archaeology at hand. It's why I take the process of publishing and critiquing the models so seriously. I'm going to lift a few paragraphs from a volume I recently co-edited with David Cowley (RCAHMS) about airborne laserscanning in archaeology, which I think can be transposed fairly directly onto my thinking about 3D modeling in excavation contexts (http://www.oxbowbooks.com/oxbow/interpreting-archaeological-topography.html).

"In particular, the last decade has seen an exponential growth in the use and awareness of ALS [substitute here 3D modeling] by archaeologists and cultural resource managers[…] The powerful images produced, all promised a brave new world. And so it is – a world of possibilities and challenges, both in ensuring appropriate, archaeologically reliable applications that inform us about the past, but also in developing practices that integrate the strengths of new possibilities in manipulation and interrogation of vast digital datasets with so-called 'traditional' skills of archaeological observation and interpretation."

Engagement with digital 3D data "highlight[s] the importance of combining 'field-craft' and observation with the powerful algorithms and visualisation techniques that dense and/or extensive 3D data demand if we are to do anything more than scratch the surface."

"In all cases the integration of 3D data into archaeological practices promotes the use of ever more sophisticated modelling and visualisations, from the creation of virtual replicas for display in a physical or digital museum or dissemination over the internet, to virtual reality and immersive visualization projects. Throughout, while the primary aim of these products may be to communicate and engage with a wide audience, these approaches also have a vital role for the investigating archaeologist in supporting interpretation where the visualization and measurement of very small scale and subtle features is essential (e.g. tool marks or rock art), and to under-pin spatial analyses such as viewsheds and least cost-paths, and inclusion in interactive virtual reality models. Universally, it is the use of 3D data as an articulation of archaeological topography that lies at the heart of the processes" (Opitz and Crowley 2013).

It was with all this very much in mind that I posed the following question in a paper I gave at the 2013 Meeting of the SAA: Does working with the models actually change our interpretations of the stratigraphy and therefore of the archaeology? This question sits at the intersection of what we do in the field and what we do in publication and as critical readers, and is closely tied up with one of the questions posed to contributors of this volume.

An Experiment

To start exploring these questions of interpretation, Marcello Mogetta (then at the University of Michigan and now at Freie Universität Berlin), Marilyn Evans (Berkeley) and Troy Samuels (University of Michigan), all members of the Gabii team, agreed to participate in this experiment. They are respectively an assistant director, area supervisor, and assistant area supervisor at Gabii, and so represent different levels of experience and perspectives on the archaeology being uncovered.

I gave them all an assignment:

1. Pick a stratigraphic sequence in which you're interested, preferably one in which you recall us having done some 3D modeling.

2. Write down in brief your interpretation of the sequence and generally

how you understand it.

3. I'll put together a model of the sequence, which we'll go through and look at together.

4. I'll leave the model with you. You can decide if you now want to reinterpret anything. Write down, or tell me about your re-interpretations or lack thereof and if you found the model at all useful.

Each chose a stratigraphic sequence, Troy picked a series of floor surfaces within a room in an archaic complex (Fig. 4), Marilyn picked another series of surfaces which intersected with a tomb, while Marcello chose to look at a series of surfaces which might or might not have been part of the road which delimits the block containing the archaic compound on its eastern side. Each initially formed their interpretation using documentation other than the 3D models.

Troy began by constructing the following stratigraphic sequence and interpretation:

"SU 3163 (Truncated N-S Wall covers accumulation SU 3165 (not photo modeled)). SU 3165 covers collapse layer 3168 (collapse of earlier wall). This collapse layer covers two patches of one yellow floor surface (SUs 3180 and 3181) and three patches of a separate yellow floor surface (SUs 3192, 3193, 3194) identified and differentiated by proximity and color. These two floor surfaces are, potentially, separate floor preparations of the archaic compound that continues across the later drainage channel (Area D Room 2). A light brown silty layer of accumulation (3202) runs beneath the floor patches 3180, 3192, 3194, 3193 and a separate grey accumulation layer (3182) runs beneath 3181. Neither 3181 nor 3202 were photo modeled. My general understanding of this sequence is that there are two patchy heavily disturbed levels of archaic floor surface associated with a wall. This wall collapsed (3168) and a later wall (3163) was built on top of this collapse on a different alignment using the debris."

After working through the model together (to get over any hiccups with the interface) and leaving it with Troy for a while, he followed up with this set of notes:

"The 3D model itself, I think, shows some grounds for reinterpretation of the relationship I originally spelled out. Looking at this model, it seems that these patches of floor are part of one flooring event, not two distinct surfaces as I originally wrote. While patchy, there seems to be a level of connectivity across the whole model with the variances in presence and elevation possibly related to the destruction/collapse levels sitting on top of these layers. This was not clear from either the interpretations on the SU sheets or from the photographs. It is easier to think of and view these isolated patches as a single floor with the model than through other means of reconstruction (drawings/photos/etc.). I think, for this specific sequence, the ability to simultaneously view the different patches was something that the 3D model provided that, outside of a brief period pre-excavation, it was difficult to reconstruct. Because these two patches (3180/3181 and 3192/3193/3194) were excavated on different days (probably by different students and certainly while other things were taking place) the model gave me the ability to look back and think about this corner of Area D in a more cohesive way."

Marilyn had chosen to look at another room from the same archaic complex, further to the north (Fig. 5). Her question was more of a general exploration, where Troy's had been fairly specific. She was hoping to better understand a complex sequence of deposits and structures. We explored the assembled model of the room together, not coming to any immediate conclusions. We did strike upon one idea, looking at a gap in an alignment of stones interpreted as a wall in the complex. This gap, we noted, lines up nicely with the central pillar in the room. While a doorway had been identified in the northern wall of this room in the field, looking at the model suggested the idea that there might be another entrance, through the western wall. Nothing concrete, but an idea to play with and think about further during the next season of excavation. Marilyn noted that the idea of a doorway seemed increasingly satisfactory, and that it is not something we would have noticed without the freedom of movement, and that little bit of distance you can get exploring a digital model.

Marcello interested himself in a later sequence, related to the establishment and use of the system of streets which structures the urban plan at Gabii from about the 5th c. B.C. (Fig. 6). He originally noted: "Below the thick deposit of silt that obliterated the entire block corresponding to Area D (SU 3004=3049), the excavators identified a layer (SU 3053) whose limits coincided with one of the roads of the orthogonal town-plan (road 2, between Area C and D). The excavators interpreted SU 3053, therefore, as road surface. The road surface covered a deposit (SU 3066) which filled a cut in the bedrock containing multiple burials (SU 3081; Tombs 41-42). The tomb is located immediately east of the precinct wall which delimited the archaic compound (SU 2219). The west niche of the tomb was dug under the wall, causing its collapse at a later stage. The stratigraphy seems to provide crucial evidence to understand the sequence of occupation and general phasing of the site, showing that the creation of the orthogonal layout postdates the burials, which can be in turn connected with the abandonment of the archaic building."

He had a whole series of questions about the sequence, which had emerged from previous seasons of excavation: "Is SU 3053 really a road surface? What is its spatial relationship (especially in terms of elevation) with the deposits that cover the rich infant burial T48, farther to the south (SU 3134=3165)? Are these road surfaces too? Probably not, because they have a stratigraphic relationship with a series of abandonment layers (SU 3129, 3128, 3117, 3115). But how are these abandonment layers different from SU 3053?"

After looking at the model, the initial interpretation of the stratigraphic sequence was revised. He noted: "The model proved very useful for the interpretation of the road sequence, especially SU 3134. The limits of this SU correspond to those of road 2, as can be reconstructed on the basis of SU 3053. The SU seems to represent a leveling layer for the creation of road 2 (in fact, it seals the fill of a ca. 500 BCE infant burial). As a consequence, the structural feature next to it (SU 3163) may represent a retaining wall for the road, not a feature relating to the archaic compound (though perhaps it was built repurposing the collapse of the precinct wall). In light of this, I would now suggest that SU 3128 is the original road surface which was packed on top of the leveling layers (in fact it also includes a concentration of pebble-like stones, perhaps the glareata?). The elevations are consistent with this reconstruction. On the other hand, I now doubt that there is a direct stratigraphic relationship between SU 3134 and SUs 3129, 3117 and 3115 (it seems to me that this depends on the fact that SU 3134 was initially considered as extending west of structure SU 3163)."

In all three cases the interpretation of the stratigraphic sequence changed,

82

in more or less significant ways, after incorporating the 3D models into the interpretive process. I would argue, based on this experiment, that if our understanding of stratigraphic sequences, those fundamental building blocks of the interpretation of excavation data, are being changed on the basis of working with 3D models, then we are already beyond 'illustrations for arguments', and I feel we can answer "yes", 3D modeling is in the process of proving itself to be an essential basis for analysis and a robust means of archaeological communication, argument and narrative.

Interim conclusions

Methodological development is messy, and the impacts of new technologies on actual practice are usually indirect and only emerge later. The personalities involved are important, because the obstacle isn't so much the technology itself but rather our motivation to use it and our default behaviors, the tools we reach for when sifting through archaeological evidence, and the interaction between those tools and our thought processes as researchers and readers. These ingrained practices, our field habits and our desk habits, don't evolve quickly. We talk about 3D field recording and SFM as new technologies. The ground on 3D field recording at a large scale was broken by people like Dominic Powlesland working at West Heslerton in the early 1980s (http://www.landscaperesearchcentre.org/), and we've had large scale SFM-based recording going at Gabii since 2009. 'New' is relative. Continued reassessment of our practices is essential, as is a willingness to go out on technical and methodological limbs. 3D modeling will only get through the 'experimental' phase of the process it becomes a tool used by the archaeological community at large for analysis and as a robust means of making an argument if we actually try and use it to do these things, publish or otherwise share the results and the process, and are willing for it to occasionally go wrong. As always, it will take time and effort for new methods to become fully integrated into our interpretive work, our writing, our reading, and our way of thinking. We continue to work within the Gabii and *21st c. Data, 21st c. Publication* projects to use 3D modeling to record and interpret excavation data, make archaeological arguments and communicate them well, and make these data become part of the "normal" archaeological record, embedded in the conversational cycle of of publication, review, critique, and response.

Works Cited

Becker, Jeffrey A. and Nowlin, J. (2011). "Orientalizing Infant Burials from Gabii, Italy." *BABESCH* 86:27-39.

Opitz, R. (2013). "Digital Transitions: Technologies for Archaeological Fieldwork, Publishing and Community Engagement." SAA 78th Annual Meeting, Honolulu, Hawaii, April 3-7, 2013.

Opitz, R. and David Crowley eds. (2013). *Interpreting Archaeological Topography. Airborne laser scanning, 3D data, and ground observation.* Oxford: Oxbow Books. (*Occasional Publication of the Aerial Archaeology Research Group*, 5).

Tukey, John Wilder (1977). *Exploratory Data Analysis.* Reading, MA: Addison-Wesley.

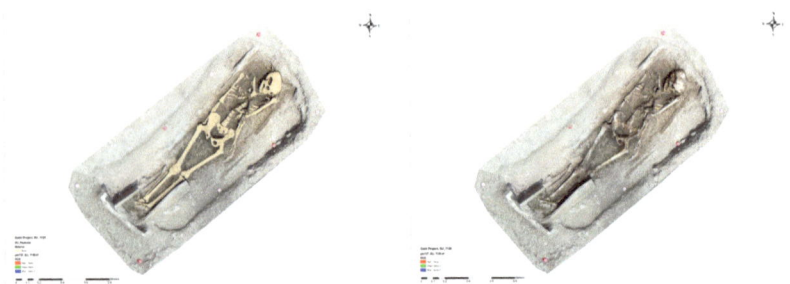

Figure 1: Detailed drawing using orthophotos generated from
3D models

Figure 2: Jessica Nowlin taking photos for 3D model creation

Figure 3: A typical single context model viewed in plan (left) and perspective

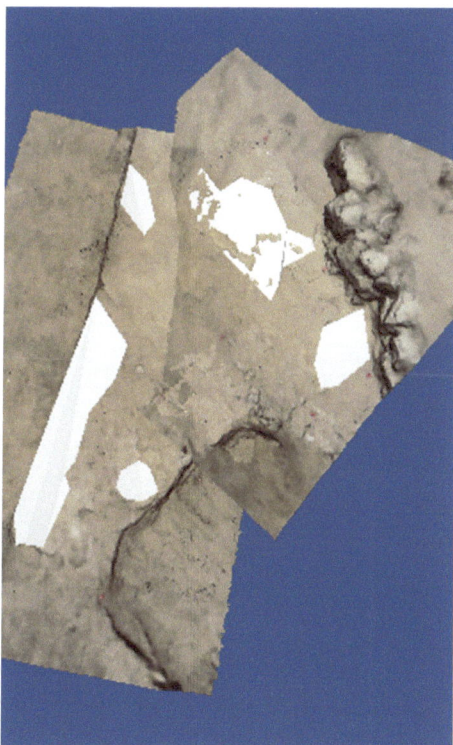

Figure 4: A screenshot of the scene put together to respond to Troy's question. White polygons indicate the locations of the surfaces in which we were interested.

Figure 5: Two walls from the sequence Marilyn wanted to study, showing the gap in the west wall.

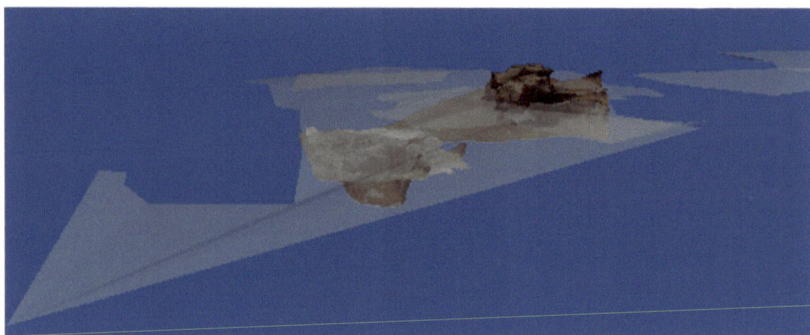

Figure 6: A screenshot from the scene assembled to investigate Marcello's question

9.
Photogrammetry on the Pompeii Quadriporticus Project

Eric Poehler

Introduction

Since the inception of the Pompeii Quadriporticus Project (henceforth PQP) in 2010 (http://www.umass.edu/classics/PQP.htm), my co-director Steven Ellis and I have been exploring the use of photogrammetry to document one of the largest monumental structures at Pompeii as part of a comprehensive digital approach to the archaeological and architectural study of this building. Our approach has attempted to integrate photogrammetry with other imaging methods, including laser scanning and ground penetrating RADAR, as well as more traditional fieldwork digital products, such as digital photography, layered vector drawings, Harris matrices, and database records. The role that photogrammetry played in this campaign has expanded exponentially over the past four field seasons (Poehler and Ellis 2012: 3, n. 6). What follows is a discussion of our experiences, our current process, and some of the pitfalls and benefits we have encountered.

Before discussing our use of photogrammetry, a brief introduction to the site and our project is in order. The Quadriporticus (Fig. 1), traditionally called the Caserma dei Gladiatori or Barracks of the Gladiators, is structurally rather simple: a rectangular courtyard surrounded on four sides by 74 Doric columns with dozens of small rooms behind the porticos. The building's original design, its evolution, and its impact on the landscape of Pompeii are, however, quite complex. The Quadriporticus was also one of the earliest parts of Pompeii to be excavated. Excavation of the building had begun by February 1767 and the clearing of the porticos and surrounding rooms continued through 1805. It was not until approximately 1817 that the great mound of debris was removed from the center of the courtyard. The Quadriporticus therefore has long served as part of both the tourist infrastructure and the tourist's image of ancient Pompeii. Indeed, by 1792 a portion of the roof and second story had been restored and toilet facilities put in place. Today, no less than a third of the more than 2.5 million people who visit Pompeii enter through the Quadriporticus each year (World Heritage Centre/ICOMOS report, 7–10 January 2013: 43) and the only signage any of those visitors will find still reads "toilets." These facts, redoubled by the constant threat of another major earthquake (Adam and Frizot 1983) that could level the site or an eruption of Vesuvius that might once again bury it completely, make our responsibility to record this building with as much detail and as much clarity as possible all the more urgent. The cork model of Pompeii, completed in 1879, stands as a testament to the value of pushing recording technologies beyond what is considered adequate for its time. With each day, more frescoes fade, more tesserae fall out of mosaics, and more walls collapse leaving the cork model as one of, if not the only, record of their former state. The ease, speed, and low-cost of photogrammetry has made it one of our most important tools to create a near-exhaustive spatial and visual recording of the Quadriporticus, a 21st-century complement to a 19th-century triumph of effort and foresight. What is more, photogrammetry can also help us preserve the now 135 year old cork model of Pompeii as well (Fig. 2).

A Digital Approach

A hallmark of the PQP is our paperless approach (see Paperless Archaeology blog by John Wallrodt: http://paperlessarchaeology.com/), for which we rely heavily on the iPad and a few key apps. At the same time that the iPad2 was released with an HD camera, we began a collaboration with AutoDesk Labs on their beta Project Photofly with the hope that that some basic photogrammetry might soon be possible in the field. Unfortunately, the iPad camera would not be suitable for archaeological photography until (at least) its third generation and Project Photofly, which developed into AutoDesk's 123D Catch products (http://www.123dapp.com/catch), required a strong internet connection to upload the necessary imagery and to download the results. The ease of making fly-through animations when the model is complete, however, remains a strength of 123D Catch (Room 7: http://www.youtube.com/watch?v=8jWWeG33gUI; Room 40: http://www.youtube.com/watch?v=oViPu8UOF7k; Room 40 with mesh: http://www.youtube.com/watch?v=ZyAu5yNZRX4). Because of the difficulty of access to an internet connection in the field, in 2012 the PQP turned to Agisoft's PhotoScan Professional software (http://www.agisoft.ru/products/photoscan/professional/). The software is powerful and, for the most part, intuitively designed for ease of use by non-specialists and students who are encountering the process and the program for the first time.

Additionally, complex subjects can be shot as component parts (called a Chunk in PhotoScan), modeled individually, and then these parts can be themselves aligned as a complete and complex whole. 123D Catch cannot offer this option and suggests that one use another modeling project, such as AutoDesk's own Maya. The power and ease of an out-of-the-box solution like PhotoScan, however, comes with compromises. At the time of writing these ultimately relate to cost. First, the professional edition costs $549 for a single educational license and a whopping $3499 for a business license. Second, PhotoScan requires a minimum of 8GB of RAM, currently twice what the standard laptop has installed. Certainly, this is not insurmountable, but one should look to see that their computer's RAM is expandable before installing the program. For running image sets at the highest density settings, however, 8GB of RAM is simply too few and processes will, after many hours, simply come to a disappointing halt. Also, because archaeological images sets can be enormous (ours are c. 300MB per room, with more than 70 rooms), it is tempting to store the images on an external drive. If a PhotoScan file is opened and the images are not in the same location (say you forgot to plug in the drive), the link to the data is broken and alignment and geometry processes must be rerun. Thus, it is best to have a dedicated photogrammetry computer.

Field Procedures and Software Processes

Our process naturally follows the contours of what PhotoScan requires and much of that process will be similar for other programs and other archaeological environments. For example, the basics rules for capturing imagery are the same and both PhotoScan and 123D Catch have excellent tutorials (Photoscan: http://www.agisoft.ru/tutorials/photoscan and 123DCatch: http://www.123dapp.com/catch/learn). For our purposes and because of our working environment, we have found that taking far more photos than is recommended to be valuable. Essentially, we "paint" the subject with a large number of overview photos and then "walk in" to detail shots, taking one or more intermediate images between these overview images and areas of particular interest or spatial complexity. Whenever possible, it is best to run the "Align Photos" at the lowest quality to ensure that all necessary imagery has been captured. It is particularly annoying when an otherwise complete model has a significant gap and although only one more image is needed, the subject is thousands of miles away. One benefit of shooting more images than perhaps are needed is that the missing part of a model might be found in the background of images of another subject. For the same reason, we prefer to add all possible images when running the alignment procedure because doing so both shows what images could not be automatically aligned and what coverage the beyond the subject was also captured (Fig. 3). Such overlap is of particular importance for aligning individual models of rooms or areas since each is a small component of the Quadriporticus and will eventually all be combined into a full model of the entire building.

Having all of these extraneously matched points, however, is not always useful for the next step in the process: building the model's geometry. Therefore, we use the cropping tool to delete these data before running the "Build Geometry" process for two reasons (Fig. 4). The first reason is simply to reduce processing time. The second reason is that deleting these data is far easier than deleting the faces that result from the build geometry process. Trimming faces is difficult enough because of their irregular triangular shapes, but it becomes especially challenging because the selection tool captures everything in three dimensions within the area selected. Thus, not only the part one wants to remove is selected for deletion, but also everything behind it (Fig. 5). This is a useful point to remember because, despite how one crops data before building geometry, PhotoScan will sometimes close areas, such as doorways, windows, or absent ceilings, that are open in the real world. Deleting these faces therefore becomes a necessary task in realizing an accurate model of an archaeological subject, particularly architectural subjects. The final process to run in PhotoScan is to build the texture map for the model from the images used.

For complex subjects like the (at least) 96 rooms of the Quadriporticus, the individual models can and must be combined by the "align chunks" procedure. Depending on the imagery available and the degree to which it overlaps, this alignment process can be done automatically by the program, or, as in our case require the manual matching of points (See Olson et al. 2013: 254, 257).

Problems and Pitfalls

The primary problem of using photogrammetry in archaeological contexts, and one that is compounded in later procedures, is the difficulty of capturing the subjects with sufficient coverage, detail, and distinction. In many cases, it is impractical or even impossible to take a picture of every part of a subject or from all the angles the program might require. In the Quadriporticus, we encountered this problem in several ways. Sometimes we could not get far enough away from a wall to get good overview coverage, at other times we could not get close enough to get clear details, and some subjects were either partially or even nearly completely obscured. The design and the scale of the building itself became an issue. For example, because the columns and much of the façades' masonry construction technique were so similar, the program had difficulty aligning these images and in the resulting model a wall would appear in the middle of a room and at an odd angle to the rest of the walls. Additionally, because of the Quadriporticus' multiple stories, when we could not get high enough to see the tops of column capitals or close enough to a three story wall. This meant that the upper portions of the building were only captured from a distance or from below, at a sharp angle.

Lighting conditions are a perennial concern in archaeological photography and this is true for photogrammetry capture as well. In the example just discussed of the high angle photos, the sun was often an issue as the sky was always significantly brighter than the wall. Many walls of the Quadriporticus (save on those rarest of Campanian summer days—overcast, but not raining) never have full sun or full shade (Fig. 6). Inconsistent lighting is a problem not only for modeling a particular wall or even room, but also for integrating that wall or room into the complete model because at different times of day (and days of the year) the shadows cast by the architecture can be radically different. For this reason, as often as possible, we took our important photogrammetry photos at the same time each day, between noon and 1:00 PM (contra Olson 2013: 252, 259). We chose this hour because the shadows were shortest even though the sun was brightest and the contrast between light and shadow strongest. With much of the southern portico completely or partially reconstructed, we also faced the opposite problem: very dark, fully enclosed rooms lit only by a small window in the door or a fluorescent overhead light. Since the ambient light from the window was insufficient to provide any detail, we chose to use the overhead lights, which meant we could not capture most of these rooms' ceilings for reconstruction.

Finally, in a building with as many visitors as the Quadripoticus has on a summer day, keeping the near background of our imagery consistent was a constant challenge. Keeping the distant background free of tourists or PQP team members was impossible. We found two solutions to this concern: 1) cropping (in Photoshop prior to adding image) or masking (in PhotoScan prior to aligning) the images to exclude extraneous features, which can give the program less to match on symmetrical objects, such as fluted columns, or 2) patience. The latter, though onerous while in the moment, is far more efficient compared to masking or cropping dozens of images.

Benefits of Photogrammetry

The comparatively low cost and little training required of photogrammetry make it worthy of consideration for any archaeological investigation and an essential tool for recording a structure as large and complex as the Quadriporticus. In fact, all of our costs to use photogrammetry to record the entire building are still less than 10% of the lowest quote we received for an equivalent level of coverage using a laser scanner.

Beyond the practical aspects of recordation, there are several benefits that photogrammetic models offer to archaeological analysis and interpretation. The first is perhaps so simple as to be undervalued: in a textured model one can examine dozens or even scores of images of one's object of interest simultaneously. Moreover, one can do this in the most intuitive of manners, by simply rotating the view like one would turn her head or body. To appreciate the value of interacting with one's data in such a manner of organization, compare it to browsing the same image set in a folder, viewing each those images individually, and opening multiple windows (each reducing screen "real-estate") to see adjacent scenes. Of far greater importance is the ability of photogrammetic models to achieve angles of viewing impossible in reality. In these virtual environments, one can—in minutes—effectively float high above or stand inside solid rock. In the Quadriporticus, the best example comes from Room 40 (http://www.youtube.com/watch?v=oVi-Pu8UOF7k), the only place where the extrados of a large sewer that served a large part of Pompeii (Poehler 2012, 110–111; Poehler and Ellis 2012, 9–10), still exists within the Quadriporticus. The digital reconstruction allows us to see through walls, examine the sewer's profile, consider how much of it supports the western terrace wall, and compare that profile to other known sections of the same sewer.

Concluding remarks

At the moment of writing, laser scanning has made the total station practically obsolete for capturing data sufficient to model complex archaeological architectures. What once took the Anglo-American Project in Pompeii and the Pompeii Forum Project several years to make only 3D wire frame models (http://pompeii.virginia.edu/), as revolutionary as they were, can now be done in a matter of weeks. Photogrammetry is also on the cusp of eclipsing the laser scanner, especially for many common recording tasks. I do not expect to see another major laser scanning campaign in Pompeii like those experiments of the last decade (Balzani et al. 2004; Cyark [http://archive.cyark.org/pompeii-intro]; Hanghai et al. 2009; Hori et al. 2007). Photogrammetry, in my (admittedly lagging) opinion, is the first step in a revolution for archaeological recordation in which new techniques will offer new levels of efficiency as well as a visual and dimensional comprehensiveness to permit new forms of analysis and interpretation. Calculation of volumes—of soil excavated for normalizing ceramic assemblages or sections of masonry for estimating the materials used in their creation (e.g., Delaine 1997)—being only one of the more obvious advances. The future will continue to experiment with both large- and micro-scale uses for recording, modeling, and presenting archaeological materials through photogrammetry. For example, features recovered during excavation can be extracted from individual descriptive models (i.e., those intended to replicate drawing of stratigraphic units) and recombined with related features to better illustrate and therefore test phasing hypotheses. Such work is already being done at Gabii as reported in this volume. Additionally, we have attempted (and thus far failed) to capture and model graffiti from walls at Pompeii, though others have succeeded on ceramics (Montani et al. 2012). The ease of creating textured, 3D images of archaeological material make the use of photogrammetry as a presentation tool one of its most potent expressions. Thus, one might photograph objects now in museums to reconstruct complete funerary assemblages and recombine them with a model of the tomb itself. Similarly, one might also use image masks and markers on pictures of frescos and mosaics now housed in museums to model the decorative as well as the spatial environment of a place by attaching those frescos and mosaics to photogrammetric models of the bare but extant masonry walls. Such reconstructive efforts are already being done for classical sculpture.

I hope that this report of our work is a modest contribution to the conversations about the place, the best practices, and the future of photogrammetry in archaeological environments.

Works Cited

Adam, J. -P., and M. Frizot. 1983. *Dégradation et restauration de l'architecture pompéienne. Institut de recherché sur l'architecture antique.* Paris: Éditions du Centre national de la recherché scientifique.

Balzani, M., N. Santouoli, A. Grieco, and N. Zaltron. 2005. "Laser Scanner 3D Survey in Archaeological Field: the Forum of Pompeii," Paper presented at the International Conference on Remote Sensing Archaeology Beijing, October 18–21, 2004, 169–175. http://www.pompeiana.org/research/22-Balzani_Santopuoli.pdf.

Delaine, J. 1997. *The Baths of Caracalla: A Study in the Design, Construction, and Economics of Large-scale Building Projects in Imperial Rome. Journal of Roman Archaeology Supplementary Series* 25. Portsmouth, RI: Journal of Roman Archaeology.

Hanghai, A., Y. Hori, and O. Ajioka. 2009. "Laser Scanning of Streets in Pompeii," in Y. Takase, ed., Proceedings of the 22nd CIPA Symposium: Digital Documentation, Interpretation & Presentation of Cultural Heritage. Kyoto, Japan. http://cipa.icomos.org/fileadmin/template/doc/KYOTO/166.pdf

Hori, Y., O. Ajioka, and A. Hangai. 2007. "Laser Scanning in Pompeian City Wall. A Comparative Study of Accuracy of the Drawings from the 1930s to 1940s," in F. Remondino and S. El-Hakin, eds., *Proceedings of 3D-Arch 2007: 3D Virtual Reconstruction and Visualization of Complex Architectures.* Zurich. http://www.isprs.org/proceedings/XXXVI/5-W47.

Montani, I., E. Sapin, R. Sylvestre, and R. Marquis. 2012. "Analysis of Roman Pottery Graffiti by High Resolution Capture and 3D Laser Profilometry," *Journal of Archaeological Science* 39: 3349–3353.

Olson, B., R. Placchetti, J. Quartermaine, and A. Killebrew. 2013. "The Tel Akko Total Archaeology Project (Akko, Israel): Assessing the Suitability of Multi-scale 3D Field Recording in Archaeology," *Journal of Field Archaeology* 38: 244–262.

Poehler, E. 2012. "The Drainage System at Pompeii: Mechanisms, Operation, and Design," *Journal of Roman Archaeology* 25: 95–120.

Poehler, E. and S. Ellis. 2012. "The 2011 Season of the Pompeii Quadriporticus Project: The Southwestern, Southern, Southeastern and Northern Sides," *Fasti On Line Documents and Research* 249: 1–12. http://www.fastionline.org/docs/FOLDER-it-2012-249.pdf.

World Heritage Centre/ICOMOS report, 7–10 January 2013.

Figure 1: Quad and context balloon flight

Figure 2: Plastico 1879 in PhotoScan

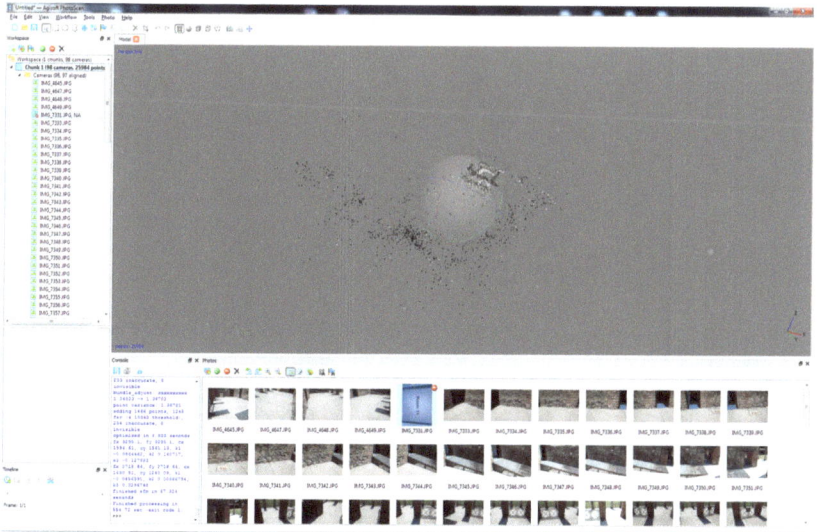

Figure 3: AlignedPhotos Overview Pixels

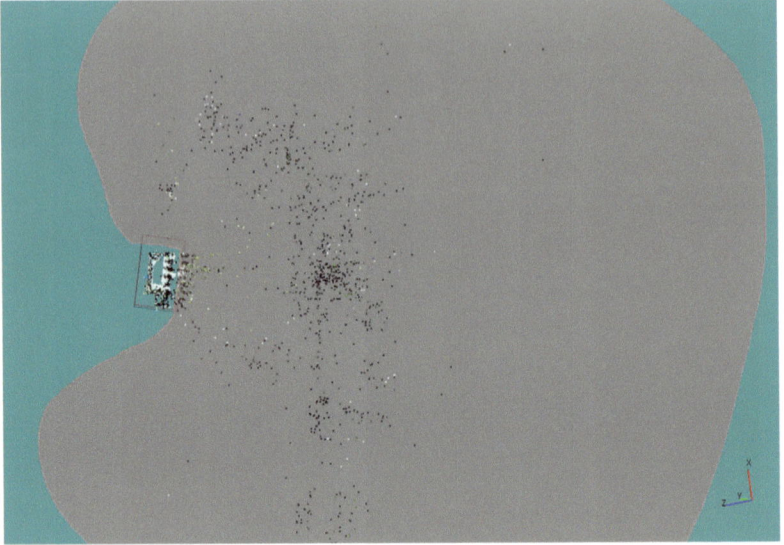

Figure 4: Build Geometry

Figure 5: Build Geometry

Figure 6: Quad light conditions

10.

3D Reconstruction of the Renaissance Bastion at the Langenbrücker Gate in Lemgo (Germany)

Guido Nockemann,

Beginning in the 16th century and up until the Thirty Years War (1618–1648), the city of Lemgo was transformed into a Renaissance fortress with a rampart, trench, and bastions, but, unfortunately, the fortifications were never finished. The southern entrance to the city was a bastion bathed by the river Bega with an associated gate construction with rampart and outer bailey on the city side (Fig. 1). During archaeological excavations from 2009 to 2011 in preparation for construction of the Langenbrücker Gate, remains of a Renaissance bastion were discovered. Excavators uncovered massive counter bearings of the former bridge, wall remains of the outer bailey, torwange, curbstones of the gate, remains of the foundation of the bastion's gate tower, wall fragments of the northern part of the bastion, and parts of the side walls (Figs. 2 and 3).

To present the results of the excavations to the public in an engaging manner, we created a 3D reconstruction of the southwestern part of Lemgo fortifications, which was based on both the results of the excavation and on historic plans and records (Fig. 4). The historical records data to circa 1646, the end of the Thirty Years War, but the archaeological evidence was problematic because subsequent phases obscured the 17th-century remains. Historical drawings of the city, however, are often idealized and do not necessary correspond to reality.

Overlapping old city maps with archaeological finds showed anomalies, which can be explained by the inaccurate measurement methods of that time. When there was no archaeological evidence for walls or buildings, their position had to be interpolated. While reconstructing the structures above ground, data from records and from drawings of the city could be used. As there are no hints to the materials used for the finishing of the fortification and buildings, no photorealistic textures were used in the model. With the press of a button, the actual archaeological finds can be made visible in the 3D model (Figs. 5 and 6).

An introductory text is essential for visitors to explain the basis of the 3D reconstruction. The main problem with that is, to a scientist, a 3D model is just one way of interpreting finds, but the general public will view that model as a fact, rather than an interpretation. It should be stressed in such descriptions that the 3D model of Lemgo is just one possible configuration of the fortifications.

The 3D reconstruction is available here: http://www.lemgo.net/fileadmin/image/redakteure/planungsamt/flash/lemgo3d.html.

Works Cited

Guido Nockemann und Morris Vianden. 2013. "Rekonstruktion der renaissancezeitlichen Festungsanlage am Langenbrücker Tor in Lemgo." in *Archäologie in Westfalen-Lippe* 4: 250-252

Nockemann, G. 2012. "Lemgo–Langenbrücker Tor; Ergebnisse der archäologischen Untersuchungen, Kampagnen 2010/2011," http://www.lemgo.net/fileadmin/image/redakteure/planungsamt/Denkmalpflege/Ausgrabung_Langenbruecker-Tor_2012.pdf

Figure 1: The Langenbrücker gate on a copperplate print
of Elias and Henry van Lennep circa 1663.

Figure 2: Southern abutment of the bridge
and wall remains of the bastion.

Figure 3: Northern abutment of the bridge.

Figure 4: Detail of a cityscape of Lemgo south, circa
first half of the 18th century.

Figure 5: 3D reconstruction of the bastion and gate system at the Langenbrücker gate
(graphic: Morris Viaden - Kleinkino / Medienproduktion)

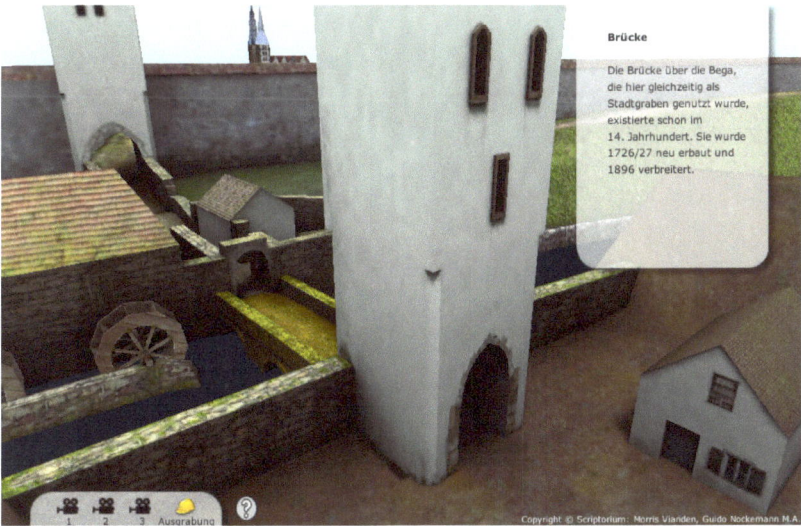

Brücke

Die Brücke über die Bega, die hier gleichzeitig als Stadtgraben genutzt wurde, existierte schon im 14. Jahrhundert. Sie wurde 1726/27 neu erbaut und 1896 verbreitert.

Figure 6: Detail of the 3D reconstruction
(graphic: Morris Viaden - Kleinkino/Medienproduktion)

11.
Bringing the Past into the Present:
Digital Archaeology Meets Mechanical Engineering

Brandon R. Olson
Jody M. Gordon
Curtis Runnels
Steve Chomyszak

Introduction

New technologies are making it possible to reinvestigate what ancient human life was like in earlier historical eras in ways that are more ethical, safe, cheap, and exact than ever before. One of the most groundbreaking technologies harnessed to analyze archaeological objects and landscapes is 3D modeling and, consequently, 3D printing. Over the last two years, as 3D modeling software, techniques, and printers have rapidly become cheaper and more user friendly, the adoption of 3D technologies in archaeological research has literally exploded with new projects appearing on a daily basis, as demonstrated by numerous contributions to this volume. Although archaeologists began printing objects created with 3D laser scanners a few years ago (Kuzminsky and Gardiner 2012; Niven et al. 2009), the speed of technological development focusing on modeling and printing in 3D presents another tool for the archaeologist's expanding digital toolkit. Our purpose here is to present a preliminary study of the applicability of image based modeling (the full comprehensive study has since been published (Olson et al. 2014)), as opposed to laser scanning, for 3D printing in archaeology using three printing formats (ABS plastic, powder, and resin). The artifact we tested was an Acheulean handaxe (Figure 1A), the same artifact presented in Olson and Placchetti (this volume).

The Problem

Efforts to illustrate accurately the form and appearance of chipped stone tools of flint, obsidian, and other siliceous rocks have been ongoing since the mid-19th century when the first flaked stone artifacts were recognized as the artificial products of early human handicraft. Photography has only

rarely been employed for illustrating stone tools because of the reflective surfaces of the rocks that were used to manufacture the tools, which
make it difficult to light the specimens adequately to bring out the texture.
There was also the problem of the depth of field, which made it difficult
to focus both on the center and the retouched edges of the stone tool in
the same photograph. Finally, the 3D form of the artifact was difficult to
evaluate in the flat, 2D world of reflective analog photography.

These difficulties were overcome, at least partially, by the use of measured
line drawings that included the outline of the stone tool, the pattern of
the scars on the surface left by the removal of flakes in the reduction and
retouch stages of artifact manufacture, and the use of shading lines in the
flake scar outlines to suggest the volume of the artifact and the texture
of its surface as they might have appeared if the artifact was lit oblique-
ly from the upper left. These conventions for making 2D technical line
drawings were established by French and English archaeologists in the
1860s, and have been used in publications ever since to enable readers to
"see" artifacts like the Palaeolithic handaxes that convinced early archaeologists of the antiquity of humans in Europe. There was even a chromo-
lithographic plate illustrating a handaxe in a publication from 1865 that
attempted to show the color of such an artifact in a realistic manner.

As a consequence of the slow evolution of the methods of illustration
and reproduction of stone tools, the demand for a more flexible method
for reproducing the appearance of stone tools has long been desired. This
need is now being met by the combination of digital photography and 3D
printing. Here we discuss our own successful experiments to photograph
original artifacts, in this case early Palaeolithic handaxes like those that
were the subject of the first attempts at artifact illustration in the 19th
century. We believe that this method, which uses commercially available
software and hardware and does not require prolonged technical training
or expensive scanners, can be readily and inexpensively deployed to the
field, whether the museum, the laboratory, or the excavation site, allowing
the rapid and accurate 3D imaging and reproduction of stone tools in a
matter of hours. In our view this is the most significant advance in the
illustration of stone tools to have been made in over the past 150 years.

The (Abbreviated) Process

The process began by taking 95 photographs at five different angles using a tripod and a rotatable surface, an effective photographic method that has been successively tested in the field (Olson et al. 2013). The object was photographed with an 18 MP Canon Rebel T4i with an 18–135 mm lens. The photos were then loaded into PhotoScan to first generate a tessellated 3D point cloud, then a monochromatic 3D model, and finally a fully photorealistic textured model. The textured model was then exported as an .obj file and brought into Meshlab for scaling and conversion to a .stl file for printing. With the assistance of Mechanical Engineering and the 3D Printing Lab at Wentworth Institute of Technology in Boston, we printed the handaxe using three types of 3D printers (ABS plastic (Figure 1B), powder (Figure 1C), and resin (Figure 1D)).

In the end, it took approximately 4 hours to fully model the Acheulean handaxe with an image based modeling technique and depending on the desired printing media, up to 7 hours for each print. From a costs perspective, the modeling of the objects required a digital SLR camera, a tripod, and a professional license of PhotoScan ($549 with the educational discount). Printing costs varied by printer type, but costs incurred for materials were as follows: ABS plastic ($58.55) (Figure 2), powder ($36.06), and resin ($120.77). It must be noted, however, that the pricing provided is based on Wentworth's 3D Printing Lab guidelines, which only include material replacement costs and not auxiliary fees that one might encounter in a commercial setting.

Implications

After critically evaluating each model, it was clear that certain 3D printing formats were more conducive to retaining minute lithic characteristics than others. The powder model, unless immersed in a durable coating, is simply too fragile for continued handling. Although the model retains faint horizontal lines, which are byproducts of printing, the ABS plastic model retained the physical characteristics that a lithicist would expect to see in a reproduction. It is the resin model that is the spitting image of the original handaxe in both its physical weight and feel.

110

This entire process has allowed us to think of all the ways that the combination of inexpensive image based modeling and printing could revolutionize existing modes of archaeological analysis, dissemination, and education, while fully acknowledging Rabinowitz's (in this volume) cogent assessments of the limitations of digital surrogates. This process now makes it possible for an archaeologist with little training to obtain a digital camera, shoot a host of photos of an object, process the images in a user-friendly and inexpensive image based modeling program, and then print a 3D model (printing costs varying between $35 and $125 depending on the material type and artifact size), all within a day's work. It is completely revolutionary as it literally brings the technology of the Stone Age back to life and solves a 150-year old problem of lithic display.

Works Cited

Kuzminsky, S. C., and M. S. Gardiner. 2012. "Three-Dimensional Laser Scanning: Potential Uses for Museum Conservation and Scientific Research," *Journal of Archaeological Science* 39: 2744–2023.

Niven, L., T. E. Steele, H. Finke, T. Gernat, J.-J. Hublin. 2009. "Virtual Skeletons: Using a Structured Light Scanner to Create a 3D Faunal Comparative Collection," *Journal of Archaeological Science* 36: 2018–2023.

Olson, B. R., R. A. Placchetti, J. Quartermaine, and A. E. Killebrew. 2013. "The Tel Akko Total Archaeology Project (Akko, Israel): Assessing the Suitability of Multi-Scale 3D Field Recording in Archaeology," *Journal of Field Archaeology* 38: 244–262.

Olson, B. R., J. M. Gordon, C. Runnels, S. Chomyszak. 2014. "Experimental Three-Dimensional Printing of a Lower Palaeolithic Handaxe: An Assessment of the Technology and Analytical Value," *Lithic Technology* 39: 162-172.

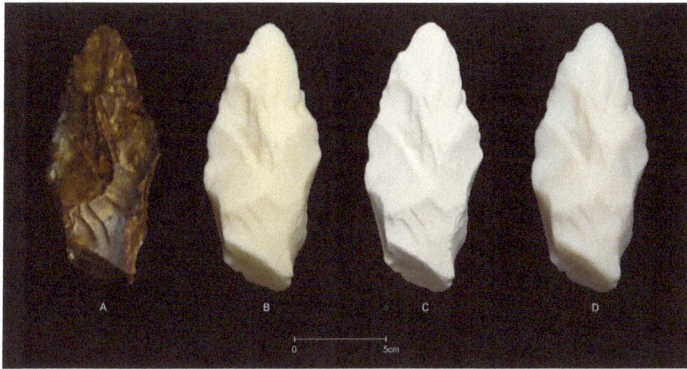

Figure 1: A): The modeled Acheulean handaxe; B): Printed handaxe using ABS plastic; C) Printed handaxe using powder; D): Printed handaxe using resin.

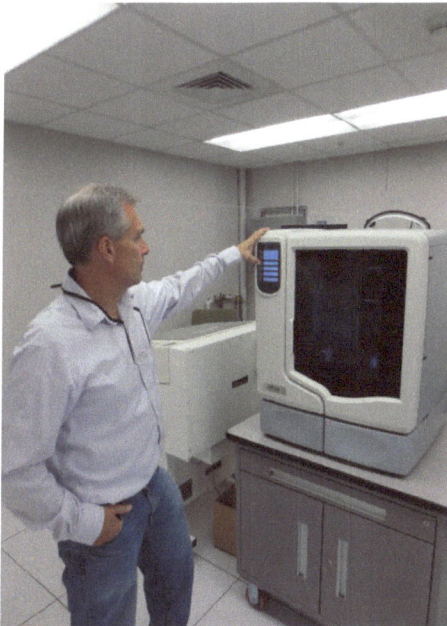

Figure 2: Steve Chomyszak using the uPrint 3D printer (ABS plastic).

About the Authors

William Caraher is an Associate Professor in the Department of History at the University of North Dakota. He is the co-director of the Pyla-Koutsopetria Archaeological Project and the North Dakota Man Camp Project.

Steve Chomyszak is an Assistant Professor of Mechanical Engineering and Technology at Wentworth Institute of Technology in Boston. He is a specialist in 3D printing and has taught a variety of classes in the Engineering Center at Wentworth.

Ethan Gruber specializes in information architecture and cultural heritage informatics, particularly focused on linked open data technologies. He has an MA in Classical Archaeology from the University of Virginia, and has an interest in 3D reconstruction and visualization, Roman urbanism, and domestic architecture. He is currently the web and database developer for the American Numismatic Society.

Sebastian Heath is Clinical Asst. Prof. of Ancient Studies at New York University's ISAW. He has worked on field projects around the Mediterranean, most recently in Greece and Turkey, and has been sharing data on the Internet since the 1990's. He is co-editor of "Current Practice in Linked Open Data for the Ancient World" *ISAW Papers* 7 (2014).

James Newhard is Director of Archaeology and Associate Professor of Classics at the College of Charleston. His most recent publications and research focus upon landscape archaeology, GIS modeling in archaeological contexts, archaeological methodology, and applications of digital imaging related to archaeological materials.

Guido Nockemann is a freelance archaeologist and also the Curator of the ISER (Computer Science Collection Erlangen). He has experience in excavations in Germany and abroad. His research interests lie in the Neolithic period and the use of statistical and quantitative analysis methods, computer applications in archeology, and the museum and collection work. Specialities: Neolithic stone artefacts and the digitization of museum objects. Intensively exploring the Web 2.0 and social media for culture and science communication, he regards himself as a "digital native".

Jody Michael Gordon is an Assistant Professor of Humanities and Social Sciences at Wentworth Institute of Technology in Boston where he teaches classes on ancient history, art, and architecture. He received his Ph.D. in classical archaeology from the Department of Classics at the University of Cincinnati and he is an Assistant Director of the Athienou Archaeological Project in the Republic of Cyprus.

Brandon R. Olson is a Ph.D. Candidate in the Department of Archaeology at Boston University. A classical archaeologist, he has worked extensively in Cyprus, Turkey, and Israel. He specializes in the Hellenistic and Roman worlds, as well as Geographic Information Systems, and 3D modeling in archaeology.

Rachel S. Opitz (Ph.D. 2009, Cambridge University) is a Research Assistant at the Center for Advanced Spatial Technologies at the University of Arkansas. Her research interests include remote sensing applications in archaeology and Mediterranean landscapes. She has participated in archaeological projects in Italy, France, the United States, and Ireland.

Ryan A. Placchetti is an Associate Researcher at The University of Pennsylvania Museum of Archaeology and Anthropology. His research addresses new developments in information management in digital environments to facilitate scholarly work and public engagement with archaeological resources.

Eric Poehler is a Roman archaeologist and an assistant professor of Classics at the University of Massachusetts Amherst. He participates in several digital archaeological projects, including as director of the Pompeii Bibliography and Mapping Project and co-director of the Pompeii Quadriporticus Project.

Adam Rabinowitz is Associate Professor in the Department of Classics and Assistant Director of the Institute of Classical Archaeology at The University of Texas at Austin. He is an archaeologist with a focus on ancient social relations as expressed through commensal practices and colonial interactions. His interest in the use of digital platforms for archaeological documentation and publication began during his work at the Roman site of Cosa in the 1990s and early 2000s, and intensified in the course of excavations in the South Region of the Greek, Roman, and Byzantine site of Chersonesos in Crimea in the mid-2000s. Since then, in the course of his preparation of the South Region excavations for publication, his focus has turned to issues of long-term archival preservation and the digital dissemination of rich contextual datasets.

Andrew Reinhard is the Director of Publications for the American Numismatic Society after serving as the publisher for the American School of Classical Studies at Athens from 2010 to 2014. He is also a Punk Archaeologist without borders.

Curtis Runnels is Professor of Archaeology in the Department of Archaeology at Boston University. He specializes in Aegean prehistory from the Palaeolithic to the Neolithic, and his recent research focuses on site location models for Mesolithic and Palaeolithic sites. He is currently engaged in the study of the Palaeolithic from Crete.

www.ingramcontent.com/pod-product-compliance
Lightning Source LLC
Chambersburg PA
CBHW040126270326
41927CB00001B/5